D1218537

I should add) don't stop the narrative, but provide little sidelights, like particularly fine views occurring during a vigorous hike. It is easy to see her emerge fully in this narrative, gaining ever greater self-confidence through her active roles as teacher, mother and, finally, as the retiring wife of the president of Babson College, leaving behind an extensive "job description" for the incoming person who would have to assume all the responsibilities Charlotte shouldered.

From the modest expectations for women in the 1950s to the most modern understanding of what it means to be a woman in the twenty-first century, Charlotte lived it all, and now you can take this journey with her in this autobiography.

—NADER DAREHSHORI
FORMER CEO OF HOUGHTON MIFFLIN PUBLISHING COMPANY

If, as Oliver Wendell Holmes Sr. once observed, "a child's education should begin at least a hundred years before (s)he is born," the trajectory of Charlotte Bacon Ripley Sorenson's extraordinary life harkens back well before her birth some eighty years ago in Cambridge Massachusetts. The Ripley name itself echoes the whispers of George Ripley and the Brook Farm transcendentalist thinkers including Emerson and Thoreau of mid-nineteenth century America.

Charlotte's memoir is a personal and detailed account of a life that plucked her from the doctrinal chill and constriction of New England and launched her into the wide, wonderful world of life beyond self. She has lived her life deliberately, navigating the inevitable cross-currents with courage, thoughtfulness, kindness . . . and the flexibility to adapt, indeed thrive, in the face of the inevitable challenges represented by children, extensive travel, and just maintaining her own identity within the context of a sixty-year relationship with her equally remarkable high-powered spouse, Bud Sorenson.

You, the reader of the narrative, will be transported in both time and geography—Stockbridge, Switzerland, the Philippines, Cambridge (again), Colorado—not as tourists, mind you, but as residents. You can almost smell the cooking. You will be introduced to those you'd previously known only in texts. You will be treated to a powerful personal perspective of events, both domestic and across the globe, a chronicle of our hyper-kinetic world.

View this as history with a heartbeat.

—STEVE SMITH
SCHOLAR IN RESIDENCE, HIGHLAND CITY CLUB,
BOULDER, COLORADO

Charlotte's Way

A Woman's Path Through Changing Times

To Margaret —
With thanks
for sharing the Path
with our family over
so many years!
Love —
[illegible]
November 2019

Charlotte's Way

A Woman's Path Through Changing Times

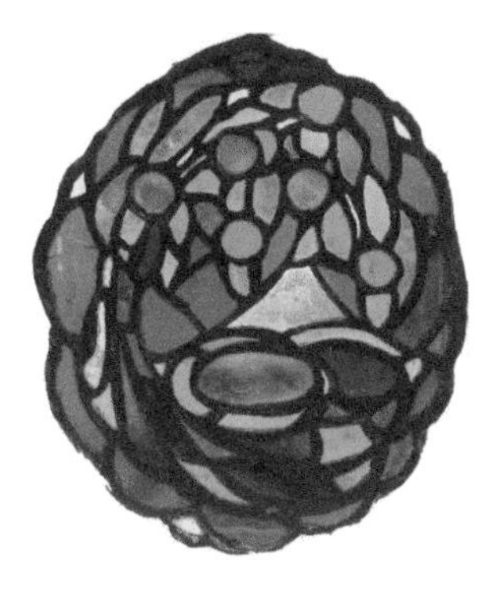

Charlotte Bacon Ripley Sorenson

Charlotte's Way
A Woman's Path Through Changing Times

Pilgrim Press | Boulder Colorado

Library of Congress Control Number: 2019913975
ISBN: 978-0-9986294-7-6
First Edition

Publishing Manager: Aaron Perry
Design Director: Maggie McLaughlin
Cover Art Director: Jake Welsh

Printed in the United States of America

Dedicated with great love to my extraordinary husband, Bud,
to our children, Kristin, Katrina, and Eric,
and to our eight grandchildren

Contents

We write to taste life twice, in the moment
and in retrospect.

—ANAIS NIN

Prologue

Rays of sun blaze through the crimson apples ripening on an ancient twisted tree. At the base of the tree, shadows darken the cobalt blue waters of a tiny pond.

This lead-bordered stained glass composition was created almost a century ago by my maternal grandmother, Charlotte Lucy True Bergeson. For me, the tranquil scene in the small oval of stained glass has always symbolized my childhood home, a secure, love-filled, and happy place. Seeing it now hanging in a window at my daughter's home near the Hudson River, I am transfixed. In my imagination, I dip my fingers into the blue water.

That simple imagined gesture releases eighty years of memories . . . of people, places, adventures, and challenges. A life story could be woven out of these memories, I think. What follows is my attempt to do just that. I offer my story with love to my children and my grandchildren.

Part One

1939–1960

Chapter One

Early Years

Lexington, Massachusetts, and Allentown, Pennsylvania (1939–1949)

It could have been snowing. There may even have been a blizzard. Most certainly it was cold when my parents, George and Ruth Bergeson Ripley, left their small apartment on Shaler Lane in Cambridge, Massachusetts, and crossed Mount Auburn Street to the Mount Auburn Hospital. At an unknown hour (no time-of-birth records were kept in 1939), I was born on the day after Christmas and named Charlotte after my mother's mother. Bacon was my middle name, a family name on my father's side.

Of course, I remember nothing of this event. I have seen old photographs, however, and know from the tender expressions on the faces of my parents as they held me that I was welcomed and cherished. My sister, Virginia (Ginny) True Ripley, was also treasured. We were called "Irish twins," as we were born in the same year, she eleven months earlier, on January 5, 1939. Only my paternal grandmother, Mabel Genevra Bacon Ripley, expressed dismay. She noted my birth in her diary: "Frigidity at the birth of the second girl." Her family was hoping, as was common in traditional Victorian households, for a male heir. Girls were thought to be more difficult to raise and, in some cases, were considered a financial burden. In the Victorian tradition, parents hoped for a male heir to take over family affairs and perpetuate and bring honor to the family name.

Our small family soon moved to an apartment on Grozier Road in Cambridge, an historic academic community on the Charles River. We moved again when I was four years old to Lexington, Massachusetts, a town famous for being a stop on Paul Revere's midnight ride. Everyone in town knew the history. Galloping into Lexington on the eighteenth of April in 1775, Paul Revere roused the town's militia, the Minutemen, stirring them to arms, crying: "The British are coming! The British are coming!"

For several years, we lived in Lexington at 73 Merriam Street in a gray stucco house with green shutters and a large screened front porch. I liked walking up the hill to Oakmount Circle to visit Robert and Grace Merriam, close friends of my parents. They were a kindly, older, childless couple who lived in a brick house with their collie dog. Occasionally, they would invite me to spend the night. I was enchanted with the little gold balls of bubble bath that Aunt Grace would dissolve in the evening bath. Sometimes in the summer, they invited me to stay with them for a few weeks near the Coast Guard station in Bar Harbor, Maine. We listened to Boston Red Sox games on the car radio on the endless drive north, always stopping to buy peanuts at Perry's Nut House. One afternoon years later when I was living in Cambridge with my own family, I came into our house to find an astonishing message from Robert Merriam's estate lawyer. He had left me $10,000 in his will. Without hesitation, I called my parents and passed the bequest on to them. The Merriams had enlarged my world. I, in turn, hoped that my parents would enlarge theirs by using the money to take the trip of their dreams. They did, leaving soon afterwards for a trip to Paris and Switzerland.

Sometimes in the spring, Ginny and I would walk about a mile and a half down Merriam Street to the local public elementary school, quite a distance for two little girls. Hand-in-hand and with the help of a school crossing guard, we would pass in front of the majestic bronze statue of a Minuteman, the Revolutionary War hero, protecting the town square.

I remember a lady who lived next door to our house on Merriam Street playing a Chopin polonaise over and over again all day long. My mother told me what she was playing and said that the lady was troubled and couldn't help the repetitive playing.

Apparently, I was a little troubled then, too. I remember going into Boston with my mother on the train to see someone who could diagnose my moods and fits. We had to walk up a metal fire stair to the second floor of a duplex in a run-down part of town. The psychologist who lived there had a big dollhouse full of dolls representing members of a family. He observed how I played with the dolls and concluded that all was fine in our family, except that my "twin" sister Ginny did everything first. She crawled first, walked first, and talked first. My parents' excitement had diminished when I reached those milestones. Prescription: do more special one-on-one things with Charlotte and praise her. I am sure I liked the new approach.

I was six on VE Day when the news came that the war in Europe had ended. It was May 8, 1945. I was playing in our yard in the small muddy frog pond surrounded by magenta rhododendron in bloom. Suddenly, there was wild shouting up and down the street: "The war is over! The war is over!" Neighbors had run into the street cheering and banging pots and pans. I knew nothing of

Hiroshima and Nagasaki and had only heard stories of the Japanese attack on Pearl Harbor on December 7, 1941. But I could feel the jubilation. I joined in with boisterous hurrahs.

From the time that America joined World War II on December 8, 1941, my father served as the air-raid warden in Lexington. He had not been called up to enlist, as his third child, my sister, Anne Appleton Ripley, had been born on March 17, 1944. Having three children excused a man from military service. Gasoline and certain foods were rationed during the war. We hung blackout curtains at night and cultivated our Victory Garden behind the house. Every household had one.

During the war years, my parents were at first charmed and later betrayed by a blond, sophisticated German couple who lived in the neighborhood. When the war was over, they learned that the couple had been quietly investigating the New England coastline searching for deep waters where German submarines could hide. My parents' delightful new friends were Nazi spies.

The war years also saw the end of my father's ten years of work at the Merchants National Bank of Boston. The reasons that he left were never discussed. Perhaps he had begun to feel that he was not cut out to shoulder the heavy responsibilities at the bank where his uncle, Alfred Lawrence Ripley (1858–1943), was president, and where the expectation probably was that in time, he would take over his uncle's position. Perhaps for unknown reasons, he was dismissed.

In any case, shortly after VE Day, we moved to Allentown, Pennsylvania where my father worked as an efficiency expert in a ribbon mill conducting time and motion studies. I remember on moving day hammering endlessly on the keys of our upright piano, one of the last pieces to be put into the moving van. I was sure that the movers thought that I was a musical prodigy, certain that my loud chords sounded at least as impressive as our neighbor's polonaise.

For several years, we lived at the bottom of a steep driveway in a rambling old house on Star Route 309 on the outskirts of Allentown. Its spacious terrace off the kitchen and the living room overlooked distant hills. I played outdoors from morning until night. In the spring, there were glens of violets and lilacs and glades full of daffodils and blossoming apple trees. In the summer, there were roses. There was a stream in the woods below the house. I would go by myself to build dams and to watch how the stream carved new channels in the dirt.

We did not have television or a record player. Sometimes, we listened to gripping dramas like *The Shadow Knows* on a big boxy radio. I saw my first airplane when we lived in that house. We all ran outside and waved at the pilot. My mother did not yet know how to drive, so we seldom left home.

One exception was dancing class. At the top of our driveway was a huge sign: Chew Mail House Tobacco. The trolley line into Allentown ran next to the sign. On days when we had a class, Ginny and I would dress up, put on our white socks and black patent leather shoes and, with our mother, take the trolley into town to learn to curtsy.

Since there were no neighborhood children to play with, we entertained each other as a family, singing, playing games, cooking, and exploring the land around the house. There were books everywhere. We were encouraged to read and to share what we were learning with the family.

My sister, Anne, must have been four or five years old when we lived there. There is a photograph from that time of the three sisters dressed as angels in the Christmas pageant that we performed for our family and a few friends. Later, we posed for a photograph in which we are standing around a large globe on a pedestal. Our mother had majored in geography at Wellesley College, Class of 1934, and loved to describe mountains and deserts, rivers and oceans, and their effect on the people who lived in different ways in far-off places. Her enthusiasm was contagious. We were fascinated by her stories. That fascination with the world has persisted throughout our lifetimes, although manifested for each sister in unique ways.

Sometimes in the fall, we would bicycle to nearby apple orchards. On one occasion, I picked an apple, bit into it and remember to this day the foul chemical taste in my mouth and the terrible headache that soon followed. In those days, farmers used chemical sprays on everything. It was long before 1962 when Rachel Carson published *Silent Spring*, warning the world of the dangers of toxic pesticides, especially DDT.

Our house was heated with coal. When the weather turned cool, my father would go into the basement, open the heavy steel door of the furnace, and shovel coal into the fire. Of course, he didn't think in those days that by doing this, he was polluting the environment and helping to hasten climate change. Those were not familiar words. We had a washing machine but no dryer. We hung all of the laundry on clotheslines, tacked down against the wind with wooden clothespins.

One winter, there was a crippling ice storm. Trees and bushes glistened with crystals. For a few nights, we had no electricity and had to sleep in sleeping bags by the fire. I remember being mortified one morning when I found that I had wet my sleeping bag. That same winter because of the snow, no one could come to my birthday on the day after Christmas. My mother was sympathetic. To celebrate, she stuck a lighted candle in a piece of fruitcake.

Several times, when I misbehaved, I was sent to my room with a supper of bread and water. I can't remember what I might have done. Maybe I had insulted one of my siblings or maybe I had displayed bad manners at the table. Until I was ten or so, my parents still held to vestiges of Victorian child-rearing principles. Children, at least when there were guests, should be seen but not heard. They were expected to be polite to everyone, especially to their elders, to say "please" and "thank you," to know how to hold a fork and a knife, and to know how to ask for the jam instead of reaching across the table. My father occasionally spanked us with a hairbrush. Spare the rod and spoil the child seems to have been the guiding philosophy of the day. I didn't analyze or challenge that philosophy. I accepted it. I was a child. This was my world.

In the 1940s, John Dewey, the American psychologist and education reformer who wrote *Education Today,* and Dr. Benjamin Spock, the pediatrician who published the influential *Baby and Childcare,* had arrived on the parenting scene with their revolutionary progressive ideas concerning the growth and development of children. By the time I moved to Stockbridge, Massachusetts a few years later, my mother had embraced their theories and allowed her children great freedom to explore the world around them.

After two years in Allentown, my father decided to leave his tedious job at the ribbon mill and move the family back to New England where he hoped to find a position in banking.

Before the move, however, my parents took Ginny and me on a trip west. Anne and our new brother, George Bergeson Ripley, born August 25, 1948, stayed with our Ripley grandparents at their summer place in New Hampshire. Called Yonder Hill, it was a white clapboard house set on a high hill north of Gilmanton Iron Works. My grandparents must have been pleased with the arrival at long last of a male child.

The trip west may have been a gift from my Ripley grandparents. For the trip, my father purchased a 1949 Ford from a used-car dealer, an unscrupulous used-car dealer. Months after we returned from our trip, we learned that we had been sold a stolen car, later repossessed by the police. Before leaving, my father signed a bundle of travelers' checks. That was considered the wise way to carry money in those pre-credit card days. He didn't realize, however, that the checks could only be cashed in certain regional banks. We traveled, therefore, on a very tight budget. I was excited to be having an adventure with my parents. The money issue didn't matter to me. In fact, scrimping a little was actually fun, as was sleeping in a tent.

My father was a member of the Boston-based Appalachian Mountain Club and had grown up camping in the White Mountains of Vermont and New Hampshire. He taught us the tricks of setting up a campsite and building a campfire. Complaining as we traveled was not allowed. On that trip, in challenging situations, my mother might say: "Okay, no more whining about mosquitos and how uncomfortable you were last night. Let's look around! Who can be the first to find something remarkable, something really unusual, something really beautiful?" As a life rule, my parents tended to ignore unpleasant matters in order to concentrate on the positive, interesting aspects of life.

We took Route 20 most of the way from New England to Denver. It was a two-lane highway then, with only an occasional passing lane. One mountain pass was so terrifying that my mother, relieved to have finished with the treacherous switchbacks, shouted with glee and tossed her shoes out of the car window down a steep cliff. I never did figure out the symbolism of that spontaneous gesture. Why shoes?

We camped out every night and visited nearly every National Park from Canada to Mexico. Established in 1916, the National Park system was fairly new, and the campsites were not crowded. We camped in the Tetons in Wyoming for two weeks while my father took a climbing course. He loved mountain climbing and joined a group to climb the Grand Teton. Because of altitude sickness, however, he didn't reach the summit, his longtime goal. My mother, Ginny, and I empathized with his disappointment.

Ten years later, in 1959, my father joined an expedition sponsored by the Explorers Club of New York. In unmapped territory in Peru, northwest of Machu Picchu, the expedition sought a legendary, but still undiscovered, Inca Kingdom. Following a native guide on an ancient Inca trail toward the so-called mist-veiled Tinti Mountains, the expedition, as described by my father, passed through territory of staggering beauty and danger marked by steep cliffs and sudden, precipitous drops into fathomless canyons. They never did find the Inca Kingdom with its golden treasure, but apparently somewhere along the way, my father discovered a lake, a rainy-season pond or maybe just a puddle, that the expedition named Lago Ripley for my father. I think that for a time, it was listed on a map at the Explorers Club. My father never returned to Peru or attempted another major ascent. He had an extensive library of mountaineering books and seemed to find enough exhilaration in his armchair reading hair-raising accounts of perilous explorations and climbs. For him, it was an escape to imagine dangling, as mountaineers did in the book, *The White Spider*, by a thin rope in a violent night storm on the north face of the Swiss mountain, the Eiger. I think that he could have been very happy living in the Rocky Mountains.

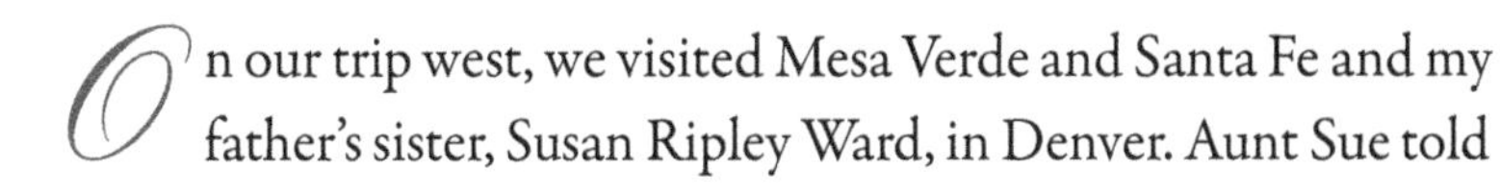

On our trip west, we visited Mesa Verde and Santa Fe and my father's sister, Susan Ripley Ward, in Denver. Aunt Sue told me that Mabel Genevra Bacon Ripley, her deceased mother and my paternal grandmother, had ruined her life with her judgmental manner. "I hated my mother," she told me fiercely. "I still hate her." According to Sue's bitter report, her mother had given Sue no choice in making decisions that would impact her life. For her daughter, my grandmother envisioned Oberlin College, then the Juilliard School of Music, followed by a career as a concert violinist. A fine life plan, I think now, if Sue's heart had been in it and if she had been allowed to participate in creating it.

For both social and economic reasons, it was important in those days for a family to marry off its daughters. At one point, my grandmother took Sue by ocean liner to Scotland to marry the Scottish minister who apparently had wooed her during a visit to New England. Upon their arrival in Scotland, however, the minister denied his suit, and Sue came home humiliated. I later learned that the minister had written to Sue before she and her mother had set sail, dashing her hopes of matrimony. At her mother's insistence, they traveled to Scotland anyway. There is a painful story of my grandmother and her daughter peering over a hedge in the minister's Scottish town trying to catch a glimpse of the wayward suitor.

To free herself from her mother's controlling influence, Sue fled to the West, where eventually she gave up the violin (she played for a few years with the Denver Symphony) and took periodic trips to Mexico where she bought long skirts and peasant blouses that complemented her dark beauty. She returned briefly to the East and married Ted Ward whom she had met on the commuter train from Boston to Andover. Ted was an uninteresting and undistinguished man who we thought was attracted to Sue for her family's money and social connections. Together, they moved back to Denver where Aunt Sue became a healer.

She was convinced that all physical ailments stemmed from one's thoughts and was specific in her analysis. "Your stomach hurts? You're repressing your anger," she would state firmly. "You have a headache? You're afraid of something." She said that she did not control what she received from the ether insisting that she was channeled by a spirit and that she had only to put pen to paper and words appeared automatically. I liked her. She was intuitive, different, and seemed to be unfettered by her New England past with its conventions, formalities, and obligations. She was certainly ahead of her time in acknowledging the mind-body connection.

At the end of our trip, we stayed for a few weeks at Yonder Hill with our grandparents. I loved spending time in the little cabin on the property that we called the Bubbalo. It was in the pinewoods on the hill behind the house and was dusty and moldy, full of allergens and mice. I once was so congested and wheezing so badly that, unsupervised and seeking relief, I ate a few tablespoons of Vicks Vapor Rub. I thought it helped.

I liked the frogs that hopped around the tiny stone mill pool and the dumbwaiter stocked with homemade strawberry jam and pickles that I could pull up from the cellar into the dining room. There was a covered well near the terrace where we often ate our meals. We would lower a wooden bucket by turning a crank, hear a splash and a gurgle, then crank up the sloshing bucket. The wood-paneled living room had a large stone fireplace and was full of worn, comfortable furniture and books. A bookshelf in the guest room was packed with paperback mysteries. I read a few, but the knife-murders and blood-saturated scenes gave me nightmares. Interior doors in the house were held open with Sears Roebuck catalogues formed into doorstops. After lunch on hot summer afternoons, everyone took naps. I read during naptime, but not the mysteries.

Colonel Harry Besse, a neighbor, had been a fighter pilot in Asia during World War II. I was horrified to learn later that he had piloted the plane that followed the Enola Gay, the Boeing B-29 that carried the atomic bomb. After the war, he became president of the Boston Stock Exchange. He kept a small propeller plane on a grassy runway behind the Bubbalo up the hill on the other side of the piney woods. He took me up in his plane a few times and allowed me to hold the controls. I was thrilled and fantasized about becoming a pilot, a famous pilot like Amelia Earhart who had disappeared with her plane somewhere over the Pacific the year I was born.

When everything had been harvested from the vegetable garden and the Queen Anne's Lace was high in the fields, we packed the car and drove down the steep hill, away from Yonder Hill.

Chapter Two

Ancestor Stories

Andover and Newton Center, Massachusetts (1949–1950)

In late August, our whole family moved in with my grandparents, Philip Franklin Ripley (1876–1955) and Mabel Genevra Bacon Ripley (1874–ca.1949). Their lovely white clapboard house at 7 Abbot Street in Andover, Massachusetts was directly across the street from Abbot Academy, a secondary boarding school for girls. Abbot itself was just down the hill on School Street from Phillips Andover Academy with which it later merged.

Since my father was out of work, my parents had been invited to stay with the Ripleys for a few months while they decided what they would do next. At some point, my mother had read in the *Wellesley College Bulletin* about a classmate, Marnie Mabie, who with her husband Gifford was running an inn in Stockbridge in western Massachusetts. My parents were intrigued. I knew that my father was between jobs, but I wondered at the time why my parents would even consider embarking on such a new and different way of life like that of the Mabies. Perhaps my parents were looking for a completely fresh start after the years in Allentown, Pennsylvania. The Mabies seemed to be doing well financially. My parents might also have thought that by running an inn they could not only earn some much-needed money, but they could keep their children busy. It could be a family project.

Already by the 1950s, Berkshire County was a well-established cultural center. During the summer months, there were thousands of visitors to the area from New York and Boston who came for the music, theater, and dance. Tanglewood in Lenox was the summer home of the Boston Symphony Orchestra. The Berkshire Theater Festival in Stockbridge and the Jacob's Pillow Dance Festival, hidden in the wooded hills near the neighboring town of Lee, were well-known. And there were other small theater groups and music ensembles tucked away among the ridges and rills of the Berkshire Hills. Culture definitely rippled the Berkshire air. In Stockbridge and Lenox, even the gas station attendants could tell you if Brahms or Mahler would be played at Tanglewood that evening and give you the name of that night's theater performance.

I imagine that the vision of providing hospitality to musicians, artists, dancers, and actors must have appealed to my warm, outgoing, and hospitable mother, a romantic with an active imagination. She had been inspired, I know, by the stories of people like Richard Halliburton who in 1925 had published *The Royal Road to Romance,* a best selling book encouraging readers to have adventures, just for the joy of it. Maybe my mother thought that running an inn could not only be a family project but could also be a grand adventure.

It could be that my father supported the innkeeping idea because he was reminded that George Ripley, his eponymous ancestor, had founded Brook Farm, the utopian community of artists and intellectuals, just over one hundred years earlier in 1841. Could he and my mother replicate that utopian experiment? Different from my mother, my father was a quiet man, an introvert. He could be curt and gruff, but he was a gentleman and a willing, considerate, and helpful host. For whatever reason, my parents made a decision to try their hand at innkeeping during the summer months, the so-called Season in the Berkshires. In 1949, shortly after the start of the school year, my parents moved to Stockbridge with my sisters, Ginny and Anne, and my brother, George.

My family was moving, I was told, but because I was thriving in Andover, I was to continue living with my grandparents and attending fifth grade in the nearby public school. I was extremely pleased with this arrangement. Not once did I feel that my family was abandoning me. On the contrary, I would have been reluctant to leave the comfortable, structured atmosphere of my grandparents' household. Even though I was not the male heir they had hoped for, and even though they were not emotionally or physically demonstrative, Grandpa and Grandma were dependable and kind. While I lived with them, my grandmother Mabel did not try to control my life as she had that of her daughter Sue.

It could be said that my grandparents lived in the manner of a prosperous, conservative, Victorian family, upholding many of the English traditions and values. Highly educated, dignified, and refined, they tried to lead exemplary lives as respectable and respected citizens who fulfilled their obligations to family, church, and community.

Life with my grandparents was utterly unlike the noisy confusion that I was used to in my own family. Their days were well ordered. Meals were served on time. Large crockery jars in the pantry were kept filled with molasses and sugar cookies. A grandfather clock in the front hall chimed every quarter hour. The clock had to be wound by hand every few days. When it had been, the golden sun and the silvery moon rose and set from the sea. I loved the chiming announcements of the time of day, especially of mealtimes.

There was a strong awareness at 7 Abbot Street of Ripley family history and genealogy. At the dinner table, my grandparents told family stories. I was never bored. I relished hearing about my ancestors and relatives and feeling that I was somehow connected to so many interesting people.

Chief among the ancestors was George Ripley of Brook Farm. George was a friend of Ralph Waldo Emerson and invited him to join the experimental community. Emerson politely declined in a letter saying that he did not think that he would have anything to offer the community. He did, however, send his nephew to live at Brook Farm. The author, Nathaniel Hawthorne, and the brother of Margaret Fuller, the well-known journalist and feminist intellectual, were also community members. Although not given much credit in history books, Sophia Dana Ripley, an educator and social reformer in her own right, was George's wife and helpmate.

I learned at the Ripley dinner table that Hawthorne had written about his experience at Brook Farm in a novel called *The Blithedale Romance*, published in 1852. He was less than enthusiastic about his life there saying that he had to work so hard on the farm during the morning hours that he was too exhausted to write in the afternoon or to participate with the other intellectual and artistic members of the community in their evening musicales, play-readings, and other entertainments.

I heard about other Ripley family connections, too. For example, the Reverend Ezra Ripley (1751–1841), minister of the First Parish Church in Concord, Massachusetts, lived during the Revolutionary

War in the Old Manse just across a small field from the Old North Bridge where the first shot of the Revolutionary War was fired. From his house, he could have heard the famous "shot heard around the world." Much later, I learned that the American educator and scholar, Sarah Alden Bradford Ripley (1793–1867) is also part of our family history. Her life story is told by Joan W. Goodwin in her book *The Remarkable Mrs. Ripley*, published in 1998.

My grandparents did not have a record player and of course there was no TV, not a common household fixture until the mid-1950s. In the music room that held both an upright and a baby grand piano, scores of entire symphonies had been reduced to sheet music for four hands or two pianos. Often, in the evenings, my grandparents would play piano duets or piano four-hands. I could hear them playing as I fell asleep. The library was full of books and folios, a globe that revolved on a stand and a full set, leather-bound with gold trim, of the famous 1912 Encyclopedia Britannica. My goal at that time was to read all of the entries. I read the daily paper, too. I remember lying on the library floor on the morning of January 17, 1950 reading in the *Boston Herald* about "The Crime of the Century," the two-million-dollar heist from the Brinks Armored Car Depot in Boston. I was mesmerized.

My grandparents employed Inez, a tall, thin, angular, grey-haired Irish cook and housekeeper. You could summon her from the kitchen by pressing a bell hidden under the Persian carpet under the dining table. In the English tradition, we ate lots of roast beef, Yorkshire pudding, and Welsh rarebit, a cheesy English dish.

I shared the servants' wing of the house with Inez. We used the back stairs and the back bathroom with the cast iron tub and a toilet that flushed when you pulled down on a chain hanging from the water tank high on the wall. My small room was cozy and full of light.

Inez was not communicative. She told no stories of Ireland. She sang no Irish songs nor danced Irish jigs. But she was proud of her small box of perfume samples purchased at the local Five & Dime. Sometimes, she would invite me into her room and let me hold the tiny bottles and sniff the different fragrances: rose, lilac, jasmine, lily-of-the valley. I was riveted on one occasion when I passed her door at night and found her sitting on her bed cutting the corns on her toes. Sometimes, in the kitchen I would help her use a mangle to press the bed linens and pillowcases.

I loved walking on top of the stone wall down Abbot Street to the Ripley family farm. Gilbert, the farmer, raised cows, chickens and vegetables. A notice in the *Andover Townsman* called the farm Rock Farm and said that it had "excellent milch cows, carefully bred." Gilbert churned butter by hand in an old-fashioned butter churn located in a small outbuilding on the farm. I made butterballs with Inez using iced striated wooden paddles. The butterballs and silver butter knives decorated our Wedgewood butter plates at meals. I learned to use crystal finger bowls, too, and pushed my linen napkin into a silver napkin ring at the end of each meal. "Pretend that you are dining with the Queen," my grandmother would say.

My grandparents' attic was full of wonders. Among the boxes of books and piles of blankets and cushions, I once found a black leather case full of dainty bottles filled with tiny round pills. One afternoon out of curiosity, I ate all of the sweet pills at the same time. I didn't realize that they were medicinal homeopathic pills, but they seemed to have no effect on me, for better or worse.

I also found treasures in the huge steamer trunks with their different-sized drawers and rods for hanging suits and dresses. In those days, individuals of an elite social class packed steamer trunks, sailed on ocean liners across the Atlantic Ocean and went on The Grand Tour of Italy, France, Germany, England and above all, Greece, the cradle of western civilization. They came home with statuary, bronze and marble reproductions of the god *Pan* and the *Victory of Samothrace*, and minds full of history and Greek myths. The European way of life, celebrated in cafés and concert halls, was a far cry from the rigid almost Puritanical way of life found in New England.

I have a photo of my father in a suit, tie, and hat sitting in the Piazza San Marco in Venice feeding the pigeons. His mother Mabel, rumpled and disheveled, sits beside him beaming in a halo of pigeons. My father looks miserable. He must have been eighteen or nineteen years old at the time. It is possible that he had just graduated from Phillips Academy and had made his critical decision not to attend college.

I walked to the neighborhood public elementary school in the fall, shuffling through the crackly dry maple leaves on the sidewalk. I was happy with my fifth grade classmates and teacher and with everything that I was learning. When I left the school in the spring to join my family in Stockbridge, my classmates gave me a special party. They wrote notes and poems and sang songs. They gave me a book, *Stories from Dickens*, and a card that they had all signed. One little boy named Jon gave me a corsage and told me that he would always love me. I saved the dried-up corsage for years.

I had one classmate who often came to play at my house. Her name was Elizabeth. I think her last name was Barrett. It didn't matter to me or to anyone in my family that she was black. We played Jacks and Pick-Up-Sticks on the kitchen floor. Outside, we played a game we called Plainsie-Clapsie. You threw a tennis ball against the garage door and counted the number of times that you could clap your hands or touch both your shoulders and your knees before you caught it again. Elizabeth lived in a small apartment that I visited from time to time near the center of Andover.

My grandfather was a gentle, quiet man. He smoked a pipe and paid bills at a handsome mahogany pre-Revolutionary War desk, sticking receipts from his grocery shopping onto a nail. I remember hearing that at some point in his life he had suffered from a mild case of polio. When my grandfather died, his obituary read in part:

> *Philip F. Ripley, deceased at his home, 7 Abbot Street, Monday evening, April 25, as he sat in his library chair listening to a radio program. Andover born, he was a type of man far too rare. Educated at Phillips Academy, Yale (Class of 1897) and as a chemist at MIT and Heidelberg, his standards of culture and character were high. His charities were many but always and unostentatiously executed. He was best known in Andover as a man of judgment, wide knowledge, probity and true to the best New England tradition as an unassuming, conscientious and splendid citizen.*

An extract from a letter received by the family at his death was also printed in the paper. It read:

> *He was so much the epitome of the New England tradition of plain living and high thinking—the noble way of life which was so nobly embodied in the Concord group of writers,*

and which, unhappily, seems so fast disappearing from our midst—so much the embodiment of that tradition that I shall always remember him as I so often met him with his market basket, stopping to pass a kindly smiling word with me about some book or idea that had interested him.

Born in Geneva, Switzerland and a graduate of Smith College, Class of 1896, my grandmother Mabel was a member of the Bacon family, a highly respected intellectual family in New Haven, Connecticut. At Smith, she majored in Classical Greek and Latin. When she married Philip in 1903, he had recently graduated from MIT. They spent their honeymoon in Heidelberg, Germany where he continued his studies. After they moved to Andover, my grandmother taught for several years at Abbot Academy across the street from her home. However, when she became pregnant with her first child, Susan, she was told that she had become "a bad influence on young girls" and was no longer allowed to teach. Until the 1960s, it was generally true that pregnancy was a barrier for women in many professions. It was assumed that a pregnant woman could not function normally or think rationally.

My intellectual grandmother was devastated. I think that it was then that she started to have migraines. During the time that I lived with my grandparents, she seemed to spend much of the day in bed in her bedroom with the curtains drawn. Sometimes, I would pass the darkened room and see my grandfather sitting silently on the side of the bed gently rubbing my grandmother's back.

There were also whispered stories that my churchgoing, well-meaning grandmother had at some point been accused of poisoning a sick neighbor. As a thoughtful gesture, my grandmother, it appears, had sent the invalid a daily bowl of milk-based custard. When the ailing neighbor died, my grandmother was suspected of having spiked the custard with arsenic. Milk, it was known, conceals the taste of arsenic.

With a population of about 10,000, Andover at the time was a small town. Neighbors knew each other and helped whenever there was a problem. The scandal filled the newspapers. Ultimately, the neighbor's housekeeper was tried for the murderous deed. My grandmother was completely exonerated. However, having been publicly named in the newspapers as a possible perpetrator must have left deep emotional scars. Perhaps this also helped to explain her migraines. Someday, I hope to find reference to this affair in the archives of the *Andover Townsman* or the *Boston Herald.*

I believe that it was after her experience at Abbot Academy that Mabel started making life miserable for her three children, Susan, George, and Helen. Being a scholar herself, Mabel had high academic and intellectual aspirations for her children, but she had little skill or sensitivity as a parent. As my Aunt Sue had suggested, her mother directed all of her thwarted energies into controlling her children's lives.

For example, she forced my father who was extremely bright, to skip the first three grades in elementary school. He was only seven years old in the fifth grade. Although he was a natural athlete and loved sports, he was so small compared with his classmates that he was only allowed to carry water for the athletes. He couldn't participate in their games. Eventually, my father was sent to the Fessenden School, a private school for boys in nearby West Newton, to repeat the years he had missed. My mother often told this story as I was growing up to help provide an explanation for moments when he was caustic and impatient. I know that my mother's respectful and tender feelings toward my father stemmed from the pain she knew he had endured as a child and young man.

As was the case with his sister, Sue, my father was judged and criticized at every turn. When he rebelled and in his senior year at Phillips Academy refused to go on to Yale, the "family" college, his mother would not even go up the hill to Phillips Academy to attend his graduation. Later, she agreed with other family members that my father should be disinherited for breaking with this family tradition. I was told that my father was incredulous and disheartened when the wills of both his wealthy and well-known uncle Alfred Ripley and then, twelve years later, his father, were read and he realized that he would receive almost nothing from either estate. This may have been retribution for my father's rebelliousness or perhaps for his failure to fulfill Uncle Alfred's expectations at the Merchants National Bank of Boston.

When I learned of this, I was shocked, but perhaps it was understandable given that producing a willing and capable male heir to help provide for the family and to embellish the family legacy was one of the foremost obligations of any family with roots in Victorian traditions. Although he left a generous stipend to his housekeeper, to his chauffeur, and to Gilbert who ran the Ripley family farm, Uncle Alfred left the bulk of his estate and his large house to his sister's son, his nephew, Tom Shipman. My mother told us these stories, but my father never mentioned these matters.

My mother was also left out of the wills. Later, after my father's death, my sisters and I who had benefitted modestly from generation-skipping trusts gave our portions of the inheritance to our mother. Uncle Alfred's treatment of my mother and father seemed to us to be outrageously unfair.

The second Ripley daughter and youngest child, Helen, whom we called Aunt H, attended Abbot Academy and then Bryn

Mawr College, Class of 1935. She was the family renegade who became a Democrat, moved to Washington, D.C. and joined the Navy during World War II as a member of the WAVES (Women Accepted for Volunteer Emergency Service). When she died, we received a letter from the federal government saying that she was entitled to full military honors, including the riderless horse and the jet flyover, at Arlington National Cemetery for having helped an elite band of women crack the Japanese naval code, *Purple*. The output from the code was called *Magic*.

Over the years, whenever we asked Aunt H what she had done during the War, she would answer, "Oh, I just served coffee to the Commander." We had seen her Navy uniform in the attic of her small house at 3227 Volta Place in Georgetown, Washington, D.C. and knew that she had been in the Navy. But she never spoke about what she had done to help the war effort. The women involved in the project had been told that if they revealed anything about their work during their lifetimes, they would be shot as traitors. This was the same threat used against the British who cracked the German code, *Enigma*. Aunt H kept her word and revealed nothing about her work. Aunt H's story can be found in the Archives and Special Collections at Phillips Academy in Andover.

Aunt H never married but lived for years with Sarah MacLennan, a distinguished art historian, whom she had met when they both taught at Miss Porter's School in Farmington, Connecticut. Their relationship, two women living together, was at that time called a "Boston marriage." They spent the winters in Georgetown, Washington, D.C. and the summers at Yonder Hill which Aunt H had inherited. There they grew and canned or froze all of the vegetables they needed for the winter.

I never thought about their relationship. The words "lesbian" and "homosexual" were unknown to me. I was in my mid-thirties before I learned their meaning. In fact, to me, the word "gay" meant happy as in *Our Hearts Were Young and Gay*, a popular book when I was growing up. Published in 1942, it chronicled the European travels of two wide-eyed young women, an actress and a journalist. Aunt H and Sal were curious about the world, active, smart, well-traveled, interesting, and good to me. That was what mattered. We called them the Intrepids.

Today, I am happy to report that the stigma that used to be attached to those who identified as gay, lesbian or transgender has largely been erased. There is a growing tolerance for gender preferences. I hear that college students are now asked on their first day of class: "How do you identify and what is your preferred pronoun? He? She? They?" It is legal now for gays and lesbians to marry.

Uncle Alfred resided in a large house at 48 Central Street, Andover, a short walk on a path through the banks of rhododendron that separated his house from that of his brother Philip. As President of the Merchants National Bank of Boston, Uncle Alfred was successful, as had been his banker father. He was known in the banking community for having taken the lead in keeping the community stable during the Depression. He was also the head of the Board of Trustees of Phillips Andover Academy for roughly forty years beginning in 1902.

Uncle Alfred never married, although he was wealthy, highly educated, handsome, and by all accounts charming. He spent time in a rambling house on Eastern Point in Gloucester with his gay and lesbian friends. One of them, Cecilia Beaux, an accomplished Impressionist artist, painted the portrait of him that hangs today in the boardroom at Phillips Andover. We have a letter from

Uncle Alfred to my grandfather, Philip, twelve years his junior, who was about to go off to boarding school. In this letter he speaks enigmatically about his life choices. *"Someday I may tell you . . . ."* I suspect that someday he might have revealed to his brother that he was gay.

There was a third brother, George, who lived in the back of Uncle Alfred's house. No one ever saw him or talked about him. He may have been an epileptic. In the Victorian world, frailties, physical and mental, were kept in the closet. You were not supposed to air the family laundry. My mother, a product of that culture, carried on this tradition with her own children. For example, when it was evident that my brother Franklin had schizophrenia, my mother never used that word. She would say that Franklin was suffering from a bad cold. "He will be better next week." I am thankful that today mental health issues are broadly acknowledged.

Occasionally on Sundays, my grandparents and I would have a mid-day meal with Uncle Alfred. His house was huge and dark and furnished with portraits, gilded mirrors, mahogany tables, heavy upholstered furniture, and treasures from the Grand Tour. We later learned that prior to his ownership, between 1853 and 1857, his house had served as the Summer White House for U.S. President Franklin Pierce, the fourteenth President of the United States, an anti-abolitionist, and a distant ancestor of ours through the Appleton branch of the family. (Isaac Appleton, 1664–1747, Ipswich, Massachusetts.) Jane Appleton was the wife of President Pierce.

Uncle Alfred has a prominent stone memorial in the cemetery at Phillips Andover Academy. It is surrounded by the graves of his relatives: the Appletons, the Aikens, the Cutlers, the Greenes, the Knickerbockers, the Means, and the Pickerings. Today, his grand house on Central Street seems small and his sizable property has been divided into house lots.

There were stories, too, of my grandmother Mabel's side of the family: the extended and influential Bacon clan from New Haven, Connecticut. The Reverend Leonard Bacon (1802–1881) served for forty years as the renowned pastor of Center Church, also called First Church, in New Haven. His powerful sermons were said to have influenced the abolitionist views and writings of Abraham Lincoln.

As a young girl at the Ripley dinner table, I was spellbound by one story in particular, an ill-fated love story involving the Reverend's sister, Delia Bacon (1811–1859). Delia was a well-known scholar who was convinced that Francis Bacon, not William Shakespeare, was the author of the incomparable plays and sonnets. She went to great lengths to prove her theory but was unsuccessful. Somewhat in the mold of Margaret Fuller, Delia gave public lectures, dramatic public readings, both in Connecticut and Massachusetts and tutored the wives and daughters of prominent families.

When she was thirty-five, Delia was embroiled in a scandalous personal drama that tore apart the town of New Haven and divided the clergy all over New England. According to the story, in 1846 at a summer retreat in Northampton, she was convinced that a young New Haven minister, a Reverend Alexander MacWhorter, had proposed to her on an afternoon walk through sun-dappled woods to a waterfall. At that time, the language of subtle gestures between a man and a woman carried huge meanings. And in those days, a man's word was his honor and his bond.

Perhaps the young Reverend picked up her lace handkerchief and pressed it to his heart. Perhaps he bent too close to her or kissed her hand or let his eyes rest for too long a time on hers. In any event, Delia was convinced that he loved her and that he had somehow proposed. Thrilled, Delia reported his suit to her influential brother, the Reverend Leonard Bacon, who then spoke with

Reverend MacWhorter. MacWhorter strenuously denied that he had proposed marriage. There were two newspapers in New Haven at the time. One of the newspapers as well as the town's clergy took the side of Reverend Leonard Bacon and his sister Delia who were bent on defrocking MacWhorter. They accused him of "slander, falsehood, and conduct unbecoming to the Christian ministry." The other newspaper, as well as the Yale faculty, took Reverend MacWhorter's side.

The case went to trial, an ecclesiastical trial, with twenty-three male ministers rendering the judgment. The concept of a man's honor was the centerpiece of the trial. Harriet Beecher Stowe testified on behalf of Delia: *"The attentions paid by Mr. A. to Miss D. were such as are proper for a man to pay only to the woman he intends to marry."* Reverend MacWhorter won. The vote was twelve to eleven. No one will ever know the truth of what transpired on the way to the waterfall, although in 1850 Catherine Beecher, Harriet's sister, wrote a book, *Truth Stranger than Fiction*, defending Delia's conduct. Tragically, thirteen years later in 1859, Delia, once praised by both Emerson and Hawthorne for her intellectual achievements, ended her days in a mental hospital in Hartford, Connecticut. Delia Bacon's story reminds me of my Aunt Sue's thwarted dreams of marrying the Scottish minister.

During the months that I lived in Andover, I would occasionally be driven to visit my maternal grandmother, Charlotte Lucy True Bergeson (1877–1957), at her home at 85 Beacon Street in Newton Center, Massachusetts. I was named after her. I called her Nana. A widow, she shared many stories of her life. I was riveted, as I had been when listening to Ripley family tales.

Like the Ripleys, Nana descended from an old and distinguished family, the Henry True family, that had emigrated in 1644 from England and settled in Salem in Essex County, Massachusetts. Nana was born in Dutchess County, New York and was a graduate of Salem Teachers College. She taught music, art, and history in several schools before her marriage. She was completing her membership application for the DAR (Daughters of the American Revolution) just before her death.

Thankful Elizabeth Jackson True (1854–1933), Nana's mother and my great-grandmother, was called "Thankie" for short. She had a peg leg, as part of one leg had been shorn off in an elevator accident in Boston. She was high-spirited and fun, according to my mother who used to visit her grandparents at 111 Elm Street in Marblehead.

Nana's father, Dr. Richard Smith True (1844–1929), had practiced medicine in Boston. In his early years, she told me, he taught Shape-Note singing in various New England communities. Shape-Notes were in the form of triangles, squares, ovals and rectangles. It was considered easier to teach people to read music in this form than using the traditional musical notation. And it was common at the time for singing teachers to go from town to town bringing people together to learn this method. To my surprise, I recently learned from my daughter Kristin that Shape-Note concerts are held in the summers at Saint Paul's, the small chapel near her summer home on Dutch Neck in Waldoboro, Maine.

Thankful wrote the *Grace* that we sing to this day at special family meals. It was written for four parts, soprano, alto, tenor and bass. I like to imagine that Thankie was helped with the harmonies by her musical husband. Perhaps the family learned the *Grace* using Shape-Notes.

Nana's house had no shower. There was a tub, but not much hot water, so my grandmother gave herself a sponge bath at the bathroom sink every day. She used golden, clear, fragrant glycerin soap. To this day, when I see or smell glycerin soap, I think of her.

Whenever I visited, I liked to watch my grandmother unpin her long gray hair. She would sit on her four-poster bed in the room overlooking Beacon Street and brush her hair slowly using a silver-backed hairbrush and holding an embossed silver mirror. Even in 1949, Beacon Street was relatively quiet with only occasional cars passing by. When my mother was growing up, however, the view from the window was different. Horses and carriages clattered up and down Beacon Street.

Although she had little money, Nana was always well-dressed in tailored suits and silk blouses. She had interesting jewelry such as a real Egyptian scarab set into a gold ring. I inherited some of her jewelry, all of which was later stolen to my great dismay.

Nana would sometimes ask me to walk to S.S. Pierce, a delicatessen in Newton Center, a block or so away. There I bought *petits-fours,* delicious little white cakes frosted with pastel flowers. My grandmother and I would then have a formal tea party, an English tradition. She had a collection of teacups and I could choose whichever cup and saucer I liked. Our family had the delicious petits-fours again when we drove in the early years from Lexington or Andover to celebrate Christmas Eve with Nana.

On September 30, 1908 in Marblehead, Massachusetts, Nana married my grandfather, Dr. John Bergeson (1864–1927), an eye, ear, nose and throat specialist who practiced in Boston. Dr. John, as he was known, also practiced homeopathy, the holistic healing method that was popular at that time. He was a compassionate man, we were always told, who refused payment from his indigent patients. "You owe me nothing," he would say, "you have suffered enough." He was beloved by his patients who repaid his kindness with gifts of homemade bread and fresh fish.

Nana often told me stories about her husband. Dr. John was born in a sod hut on a farm in Earlsville, Illinois. Before moving to America, Ole Bergeson, John's Norwegian father and my maternal great-grandfather, lived on a steep north-facing mountainside farm on the Ardahlfjord, part of the Stavangerfjord on the southwest coast of Norway. Madly in love with beautiful Rakel Runestad who lived across the Ardahlfjord on the sunny island of Fogn, Ole thought nothing of rowing seven kilometers across the fjord to court her on her farm.

After they married, Ole built a fifty-foot wooden boat called a *jekt* on the pebbly beach below his farm. In the mid-1800s when the Norwegian fishing economy was collapsing, hundreds of thousands of Norwegians emigrated from Norway to America. In 1857, Ole sailed in his jekt with Rakel, his children, and other Norwegian emigrants to Montreal. From there the Bergeson family made its way to Illinois.

In the summer of 2017, with members of my family, I visited the farm belonging to Ole Bergeson and saw the beach on which Ole had built his boat. On another day, we took the ferry to the beautiful island of Fogn, Rakel Runestad's home. In each place, we were fortunate to be welcomed by distant relatives.

My grandfather John, the son of Rakel and Ole, was an outstanding student who attended the University of Iowa, then traveled to Paris to study medicine at the Sorbonne. In the late 1800s, Paris was the only city in the world where one could receive an excellent medical education. I like to imagine this mid-western farm boy arriving in Paris with its spacious parks, monumental buildings, cathedrals and cafés, and broad boulevards filled with horse-drawn carriages.

Dr. John loved the rich cultural life in Paris, especially the opera. Wearing a top hat, he would attend the opera with his friend, Stanislov, a Polish aristocrat who as a teenager and with only a few minutes warning had escaped from Poland and a Russian invasion. My grandfather stayed in Europe for seven years. By the time he left, he had been trained as an eye, ear, nose, and throat specialist. He was also fluent in five languages.

When Dr. John returned to Illinois, the local Native American chief offered him his daughter in marriage. Dr. John went to Boston and married Charlotte Lucy True instead.

Hanging in our house in Cambridge is a portrait of my grandfather painted in 1895 in Paris by the Impressionist painter, Jules Fachnlein. I love the portrait with its somber tones and touches of red. My grandfather appears to be a kind, thoughtful man with great natural dignity. From all accounts, he had a happy heart, loved people, and made them laugh. I like to think that my mother resembled her father with her love of people, her open and generous heart, her playful imagination, wit, and free spirit. And her love of cafés! She must have been enchanted by her father's stories of Parisian life.

My grandfather died from lead poisoning in 1927 at the age of sixty-three. He had been cooking his breakfast eggs in the special skillet that he had brought with him from Paris. The skillet contained lead. My mother was fourteen when her father died. She adored him, and his death broke her heart. She never got over it, her eyes filling with tears whenever his name was mentioned.

When I look at Nana's stained glass apple tree and the little pond mentioned at the beginning of these remembrances, I wonder why my grandmother continued to work with lead after the death of her husband. I guess not much was known at the time about its insidious danger in cookware, crystal goblets, water pipes, gasoline, paint, and stained glass. Laws against using lead-based paint weren't passed in the United States until 1978.

Because of Dr. John's generosity with regard to his patients, he left his family with a relatively small inheritance. Nana struggled economically as a widow with three children to raise and educate. She earned money by teaching school and by painting and selling beautiful trays with stunning motifs of pumpkins, flowers, and vines copied from the Japanese scrolls and screens that she sketched at the Museum of Fine Arts in Boston. Her modest earnings required that the family live frugally.

One rainy evening after her husband's death, so the story goes, her front doorbell rang. A gentleman in a hat and tan overcoat was at the door. My mother was sitting on the front stairs and overheard the gentleman, Mr. Alfred Sawyer, say to my grandmother: "I know, Mrs. Bergeson, how hard life has been for you. I admired your husband and I admire you. I am providing you with enough money so that you will be able to send your three children to college. It is my gift to you. Please do not feel indebted."

My mother, Ruth Bergeson, went to Wellesley College, Class of 1934, Uncle John to Brown University, Class of 1936, and Uncle Lloyd to MIT, Class of 1938. All three attended these excellent colleges, kindness of Mr. Sawyer. I think that he was a successful Boston investor. I wish I knew more about him.

My grandmother influenced my life in many ways. I majored in Art History at Wellesley College because of Nana. When I visited her, I used to lie on the carpet in the room with the upright piano and leaf through her wonderful collection of art books and folios. I was beguiled by the paintings of Fragonard, Watteau and Chardin and intrigued but baffled by the innumerable paintings of Christ's crucifixion with their wretched, bloody scenes depicted on gold backgrounds.

Nana loved to garden. I remember her delight at the glowing pastel colors of the spring foxgloves and the delphinium. And her pleasure in the strong scents of lilacs, mock orange, honeysuckle, privet, peonies, and roses. I think that I inherited my love of flowers and gardening from her.

Perhaps she is the one who gave me *Gabriel and the Hour Book*, my favorite book during my early years. It was the story of a young boy growing up in a monastery in the Middle Ages who was trained to illuminate the borders of medieval manuscripts with flowers, butterflies, and bees. Gabriel's paint colors came from the plants and minerals that he collected and ground up into powder.

My grandmother often took me to visit both the Boston Museum of Fine Arts with its Japanese temple and garden and the nearby Isabella Stewart Gardner Museum with its glorious, flower-filled interior courtyard with the Roman mosaic floor. Nana and I would make the trip from Newton Center to Boston in her little black Ford. I rode in the rumble seat. There was not much traffic in those days, so it was perfectly safe to drive with the top down and no safety belts. I was fortunate later in life to be able to give some financial help to the Gardner Museum to support its annual April display of nasturtiums cascading from the balconies above the courtyard garden.

Not anticipating that I would one day attend Wellesley College, Nana and I sometimes drove to visit the beautiful campus. We would walk down to the shore of Lake Waban and sit in a secluded spot on Tupelo Point. It was then that I got the idea of establishing a meditation retreat on the shore of that lovely lake. With the support of Diana Chapman Walsh, the President of Wellesley College, I was fortunate once again later in my life to be able to fulfill that dream. The granite meditation retreat for which I made the original design is located in a tranquil spot on Lake Waban in front of the Slater International Student Center. I think that my inscription, "*In Stillness There is a Song*," fits the surroundings. In that natural setting, the words can be understood on several levels.

On a recent spring afternoon when I was leaving the retreat, I turned and saw a few Muslim students wearing head scarves entering the retreat. *That's perfect,* I thought. *Maybe the inscription is short enough and universal enough in its imagery that these young women will carry it in their minds and hearts when they return from Wellesley to their homes in the Middle East. Maybe reflecting upon the inscribed message will help them somehow in their lives.*

My grandmother Nana was a serious, dignified woman, highly principled with a profound sense of duty. I admired her refinement and good taste. However, as far as I was concerned, she lacked both personal warmth and a sense of humor. My mother found Nana, her own mother, to be judgmental and overbearing. I later wondered why, even though I was her namesake, she had never given me a hug.

Chapter Three

Growing Up

Stockbridge, Massachusetts, and Pilgrims Inn (1950–1960)

In the early spring of 1950 during my fifth grade year, I received a letter from my mother. She was full of excitement writing that I was to join the family in Stockbridge. I was to come before the end of my school year in Andover. Her letter read:

> *We are fixing up the icehouse of an old farm. Actually, sheep lived in one end of this small building. They used to cut blocks of ice from a nearby lake and keep the blocks in sawdust in the room at the other end. There is moss on the roof and a tree growing through the ceiling of the living room. When you first come and until we are ready to move in, we will be living nearby with the Mabies at Christmas Tree Inn. They have nine children.*

I was alarmed, in fact devastated, when I read the letter. I remember sobbing. I was attached to my quiet, ordered life with my grandparents. What my mother described didn't sound at all enticing. It sounded like mayhem. But I had no choice. The decision had been made. On a cold gray morning in early May, soon after my classmates had given me a farewell party, my dignified grandfather and I boarded a Peter Pan bus in Boston's South Station. The road going west into the Berkshire Hills was a two-lane road that twisted and turned and finally wound up and over what was called Jacob's Ladder. As I recall, the trip took most of the day. I had motion sickness and was sick to my stomach. Travelers complained because of the smell, and my grandfather and I were asked to leave the bus and wait for another. It was snowing gently, a light spring snow, as we waited for an hour or so on the side of the road. I carried with me a gift from Inez, her little box of assorted floral perfumes.

I remember nothing about our arrival at the bus stop in Lee, the town adjacent to Stockbridge. I think that my patient grandfather having fulfilled his duty and returned me to my family probably took the next bus back to Boston and Andover. My father must have picked me up.

It was dark when we arrived at Christmas Tree Inn. No one was awake. In fact, there were no available beds. My father took me to the small woodshed attached to the back of the inn. It was neither insulated nor heated. A cold wind whistled through the cracks in the ceiling and between the wallboards. I don't know what I slept on. It was not a real bed, of that I am certain. Maybe it was just a wide solid plank. My father covered me with a blanket and, exhausted from the day's journey, I slept.

I was freezing when I woke up the following morning. My blanket was covered with a dusting of snow that had blown in through the cracks in the ceiling and the wallboards. When I found that the liquid rose and lilac and lily-of-the-valley in my treasured perfume bottles had frozen, I began to cry. That first night in Stockbridge with my family was worse than I had imagined it could possibly be.

I don't remember much about the time that our family spent living with the Mabie family, except for wild games of tag and hide-and-seek and "sardines." No one studied nor did homework. No one read books. Circadian rhythms replaced the grandfather clock's dependable chiming. We woke up with the sun and went to bed when the sun went down. Meals were not on time or sit-down affairs. You ate, if there was enough, on the fly. Sometimes there were no meals at all. Dinners were mostly from cans: Boston baked beans, corned beef hash, or sometimes Spam, a wartime staple. Ketchup covered everything.

We had our run of the restaurant kitchen and its supplies. We liked to make a cinnamon spread for our toast. A pound of butter mixed with two pounds of white sugar plus a large tin of powdered cinnamon. We toasted whole loaves of soft, white Wonder Bread, piled on our cinnamon spread and feasted. Occasionally, however, there would be a call to a group meal: "Gifford, Gordon, David, Curtis, Katharine, Peter, Richard, Steven, Faith, Ginny, Charlotte, Anne, George, LUNCHEON!"

The morning of my first day in Stockbridge I learned that the Mabies had owned three neighboring inns—Christmas Tree Inn, Mistletoe Manor, and Holly Wreath Inn—all fronting on East Street (or Route 7, as it is now called). My parents had purchased twelve acres which included the Holly Wreath Inn with its small icehouse, as described by my mother in her letter to me. The large barn across Devon Road also came with the Inn. I imagine that my Ripley grandparents must have helped with the purchase.

Two miles from the center of Stockbridge, on the northeast corner of Route 7 and Devon Road, Holly Wreath Inn was a sprawling New England white clapboard farmhouse with rooms that had been added over many generations to the original building. Originally, the Inn had been called the Halfway House, as it was situated halfway between the towns of Great Barrington and Pittsfield. It had also been a stop in the early years on the stagecoach route from Albany to Boston. As proof, there was a rusty, weathered abandoned stagecoach next to the barn. I played in the decrepit stage for hours imagining hold-ups by lawless brigands and Indians. I imagined that a beautiful woman dressed in taffeta and wearing kid gloves and a feathered hat with a veil was always huddled inside, terrified.

Besides being a cultural mecca, visitors were also attracted to the area by the many mansions, called Berkshire Cottages, built at the turn of the century before the 1913 creation of the federal income tax. Wealthy families with their servants would come from Boston by car or from New York City by train to spend summers in the Berkshires Hills. The air was fresh, and you could wear white, carry parasols, and play tennis, golf and croquet. Or you could sail and canoe on Lake Mahkeenac or the Stockbridge Bowl, as it was called by the locals. The Berkshire Cottages vied with the mansions in Bar Harbor, Maine or Newport, Rhode Island and other cool, scenic spots. The story goes that the son of Mr. and Mrs. Anson Phelps Stokes who owned Shadowbrook, a Berkshire Cottage overlooking the Stockbridge Bowl, wanted to invite ninety-seven of his Yale College classmates to spend the weekend. His mother admonished her son, "Don't invite more than fifty. We already have guests." Shadowbrook burned down in 1956. The site, which for a time housed a Jesuit novitiate, is currently owned and operated by the Kripalu Center for Yoga and Health.

Later in the spring of 1950, our family of six moved from Christmas Tree Inn into what became known more formally as the Icehouse. When I first saw our new home, the tree growing through the roof in the living room had been removed. The living room still had a dirt floor, however, and there was still moss on the roof. But at least, I thought, the house has walls and a roof to keep out the wind, rain and snow. The front door was painted the warm color of bittersweet.

There were four small rooms on the second floor, each with a window. We children shared the tiny bathroom with a shower stall at the end of the hall. Each of us could choose the wallpaper we wanted for our room. I chose a brownish one covered with grandfather clocks probably because the clocks reminded me of my sober and predictable life in Andover.

My parents slept on the first floor at the end of the building where blocks of ice had once been stored. The space above their ceiling was unfinished. Once while playing hide and seek in that space, I stepped on an unfinished portion of the floor between two beams. The ceiling gave way and I ended up dangling over my parents' bed, held up only because I clung desperately to the beams.

Using tar as the adhesive, I helped my father install green linoleum tiles on the living room floor of the Icehouse. The living room was the space that had formerly housed sheep. I also helped him shingle the roof. When we had finished tiling the living room floor, my father hung a swing from the living room ceiling. I can't imagine why my parents thought that would be a good idea.

The swing increased the circus feel of the house. The swinger had every advantage, fast or slow, high or low. The rest of us had to keep out of the way or get hurt. Of course, we argued over whose turn it was to be on the swing.

As children, we teased each other mercilessly and argued not only about the swing but about such matters as who deserved the most homemade cookies. There were never enough. And there was never enough nutritious food. Not only did my mother have no interest in cooking, but there was no place in the area at that time to buy fresh produce. While today, near Stockbridge, you can find fresh, locally-sourced organic produce, many of our meals at that time were from cans, even vegetables, heavily salted, and fruit slices in thick sugary syrup. A butter substitute came in plastic pouches. The pouch had a capsule on the top containing yellow dye. You popped the capsule and massaged the yellow dye into what was probably Crisco.

In the tiny kitchen, my mother often made two meals that I remember. One was a spaghetti casserole with a base of bacon fat, onions and green peppers. The other was a succulent curry dish called Country Captain from the *Joy of Cooking*. As far as I can remember, that was the only page in the cookbook that had been turned down and was spattered with tomato sauce.

When my mother discovered Bird's Eye frozen peas, we had frozen peas with almost every meal. We later bought a freezer that we stocked with packages of frozen peas and some dead rattlesnakes that my intrepid younger brother George had stalked and killed on Rattlesnake Mountain, just across Route 7.

In the early 1950s, my mother somehow learned of and became interested in the revolutionary ideas of nutritionist Adelle Davis, who urged her readers to avoid hydrogenated and saturated fats and sugar, and Gaylord P. Hauser, author of the best-selling,

Look Younger, Live Longer. Often, to get an energy boost in the afternoons, my mother ate his suggested concoction of yogurt, powdered skim milk, wheat germ, brewer's yeast, and blackstrap molasses, topped with a walnut.

We did everything in the living room with the green linoleum floor. We had our impromptu meals, always candlelit, on the same table where we did our homework and put together school projects or laid out the patterns for skirts and petticoats. I hemmed the starched crinoline petticoats, aprons, and dresses there that I had made upstairs on the Singer sewing machine. You had to pump foot pedals to make it run.

During my first few weeks in Stockbridge, I felt melancholy. I was homesick for my school friends and for my life in Andover. All of the activity and confusion in our small house was exhausting. I was sometimes overwhelmed by having constantly to compete with my siblings for attention. I tried to understand why my parents had sent for me before the end of the school year. Was it their wish that the family be together before the move into the Icehouse? Perhaps they wanted me to meet children at my new school whom I could get to know over the summer. Or did my grandparents no longer want the responsibility of caring for me?

To cheer me up and give me a vision of the happy girl that I could become, my mother cut a picture of a skating girl from the *Woman's Day* magazine. The young girl was dressed in red with white figure skates. She was skating on one skate, arms outstretched, her other leg lifted in the air behind her. She was smiling and radiantly happy. It was an inspiring image. I still have it. It's interesting how one's life can be influenced by something as simple as a magazine photo, the picture serving for years as a visual mantra. Seeing, however, that I was still withdrawn and sad after a month or so, my mother organized a party for me, a belated birthday party. To help me celebrate, she invited children from my new fifth grade class as well as a bird expert from the nearby bird sanctuary.

On the appointed morning, I was awakened at six by a chorus of "Happy Birthday" below my window. I ran downstairs and joined a group of enthusiastic fifth graders. Off we went down Devon Road, the dirt road in front of our house, to the swampy area at the bottom of the hill. The peepers were just beginning to sound their raspy mating calls and red-winged blackbirds swooped about and sang. Skunk cabbages were thrusting out of the damp earth and pussy willows and marsh marigolds were in flower. It was a memorable day. I was happier in Stockbridge after that.

My brother Franklin Lawrence Ripley was born while we were living in the Icehouse. He was twelve years younger than I and was the last of the five Ripley children. I was awake at midnight on January 1, 1952 when I learned that he had been the first baby born in the new year in Berkshire County. Remembering the VE Day celebration, I grabbed a pot and a metal spoon, went outside and filled the dark, empty countryside with raucous banging.

My parents called their inn Pilgrims Inn in honor of Chaucer and the lusty fourteenth-century pilgrims of *The Canterbury Tales*. My mother was definitely not interested in attracting pilgrims of the puritanical ilk, burdened with heavy traditions and formalities. My mother, like Epicurus, the fourth-century B.C. philosopher, wanted to attract pilgrims who were jovial and merry while searching for Truth and Beauty. She drew a silhouette of a small pilgrim with his staff. The pilgrim was enlarged and painted onto the Pilgrims Inn sign. The pilgrim silhouette was also featured on the front of a brochure that captured her vision.

Whether you come by foot or by horse, by train or by car, you will find rest and refreshment in this rambling old house on the Stockbridge-Lenox Road. For the weary traveler, the bed is of the softest. The rooms are airy and gay with chintz. Baths, sparkling clean, are private and semi-private. Rooms are equipped with comfortable chairs and lamps. Some have fireplaces.

Many Pilgrims come for the great Tanglewood Festival and stay for the last week in July and the first two weeks of August. Many Pilgrims come for the plays that Billy Miles brings from Broadway to the Berkshire Theater Festival. Many Pilgrims come for Ted Shawn's dance festival at Jacob's Pillow. We welcome them all.

But the Pilgrims we love the best are the Pilgrims who come to rediscover the natural beauties of the Berkshires. We love the Pilgrims who come in the Spring to watch the world burst into bloom and in the Fall when the trees are aflame. We like to see them return refreshed after a day in the open, exploring old trails and lumber roads.

For the more sophisticated Pilgrim, there is the Drama School, the Music School, the Art School, and the School of the Dance, all within easy driving distance. The Inn itself has an interesting collection of local handicrafts.

We serve our guests a Continental breakfast, buffet style in a sunny breakfast room—or out on the grass under the birch tree—or on a tray in your room. Afternoon tea will be served every day.

We were proud of our old New England house. Above the dirt floor in the basement, the date 1798 had been chiseled into one of the wooden beams. The house had been built only twenty-three years after the start of the Revolutionary War. The floorboards in some of the rooms were between twelve and sixteen inches wide, proof of the age of the house. There was an attic where my father kept an heirloom antique Civil War sword and a pair of epaulettes.

We worked hard to get Pilgrims Inn ready for summertime guests. The Inn would not be open in the winter. There were ten bedrooms. We could take twenty guests. I will never forget the breathless excitement we felt when the beds had been made, especially in what we called the bridal suite with its fireplace, private bath, and balcony. Bright chintz curtains framed the windows. There were fresh towels in the bathrooms. The Pilgrims Inn sign had been hung on Route 7. We were open for business.

My mother was clearly the inspiration behind Pilgrims Inn. "Booma," as we later called her, welcomed everyone she met with warmth and interest. You knew that she was nearby when the air rang with laughter. She was a sensitive, empathetic, witty, and intelligent conversationalist, always eager to learn from others about their lives and experiences. She was totally present when she spoke with you, leaning forward, nodding, encouraging.

Now that I think about it though, certain topics seemed to have been taboo: politics, money, one's personal health issues, and sex. It was just accepted that those were topics that well-bred people did not discuss in company. On the topic of sex, she once found me, a young girl, maybe age fourteen, reading *The Cradle of the Deep*, an erotic description of a young woman who had gone to sea on a freighter full of sailors. My kind, and I assumed tolerant, mother seized the book and tore it to shreds in front of me. I wonder how she explained that to Polly Jones, the town librarian. It is clear that even in the 1950s, my parents still made puritanical efforts to suppress natural curiosity about sex.

My sisters and I were never given a talk about the birds and the bees. In fact, I had no idea what menstruation was or its significance until I was thirteen. My mother called it "the curse." I actually thought that it must be a curse in the sense that it seemed to put an end to my carefree childhood. Children today don't have to wait to learn about sex from their parents. Sexual images are everywhere: on television, in the movies, on computers and smart phones. I wonder sometimes if this early sexual saturation is healthy.

Grousing and grumbling were not acceptable behaviors in our family. We had all read *Pollyanna: The Glad Book*, that enjoined readers to find something positive and uplifting in every situation. We were supposed to *brighten the corner where you are*, a popular saying of the day. We were often reminded to count our blessings.

My mother loved celebrations. As a family, we celebrated everything. We celebrated everywhere. We celebrated achievements and events small and large with laughter and singing. We celebrated in the sunshine and every night at the kitchen table by candlelight. We celebrated when family members and guests arrived and when they left. We did not celebrate, however, with smoked salmon, gourmet snacks, and fine wine. Lively conversations and laughter were more important than fine food. I remember feasting during these celebrations on salty Wheat Thins and Triscuits with chunks of cheddar cheese.

At some point, my mother was blackballed from a ladies' club in the neighboring town of Pittsfield. She was deeply hurt and felt that the ladies had rejected her because she ran an inn, a business. I felt it was because, unlike most of the stifled and uptight women of the 1950s, my mother was a free spirit who added magic and sparkle to the lives of those around her. She was too original and too whimsical for the Pittsfield ladies. I hated to see her suffer from the rejection, though, and I was protective of her for the rest of her life. Because I felt that clubs with their cliques could potentially be exclusionary, I was watchful at gatherings at the Lenox Club and the Mahkeenac Boat Club of which she was a member.

While my mother might have been the inspiration for Pilgrims Inn, my father, George Ripley, was fully supportive of the effort. As a Yankee, my father had a strong sense of duty. As time went on, however, and there were more children to care for and increased financial responsibilities, he often seemed tense and stressed. Bringing up five children without much help or money was not easy, but he was committed to his family. Like many Yankees, he was stoical and willed himself to fulfill his obligations. I think that my father found release for his stress and frustrations in his games of golf, tennis, and croquet. He was an unrelenting competitor, even when playing board games with his children. He could finish Sunday's *New York Times* crossword puzzle within an hour. He would retreat sometimes to a quiet corner to read his mountaineering books.

Although money was always an issue, even after my father had found a banking job in Pittsfield, the highest priority for my parents was ensuring that their children had a good education. With scholarships and loans, they sent all five children both to private high schools for at least two years and then to college. Their daughters, they felt, should have an education equal to that of their two sons.

It is interesting that today, in countries around the world where young girls have been denied an education, there is a growing realization of the importance and value of educating girls. *Educate a girl and you educate a village* is now commonly understood by policymakers. Young boys, it has been noted, often leave their villages to make their way in the world. There is a greater chance that educated young women will stay in the village and work as nurses and teachers and in other ways create a better life and future for their communities.

In 1956, at the close of the summer season, my parents decided to spend winters living in Pilgrims Inn rather than in the Icehouse. There were seven of us, and we five children were growing and needed more space. Now each of us had a large bedroom and either a private or a shared bath. I had a beautiful sunny room with wide floorboards and a balcony at the front of the house.

We were happy living in Pilgrims Inn, even though the house was drafty and chilly. Cold air seeped in and around the ill-fitting doors and windows. There were six large fieldstone fireplaces. During the late eighteenth and early nineteenth centuries, the owners probably chopped enough wood to heat the house. We used the fireplaces for atmosphere. We heated the house with oil. There were cast iron radiators in each room.

During the long, cold winter months, I remember my mother crying softly at the kitchen table in the mornings when my father drove off in their only car for his work at the bank. He always left early giving himself time to stop for a few minutes at his favorite breakfast spot. I know that my mother felt abandoned and lonely during those mornings, left to care for five growing children and isolated from the community in Stockbridge. She missed her husband, her helpmate and companion. I hated to see her cry.

An upright piano with ivory keys was in the large front room. My sister Ginny, an accomplished pianist, would often accompany our hearty renditions of "The Pirate King" from Gilbert and Sullivan's *The Pirates of Penzance*. Or she would play the piano part of Haydn's *Toy Symphony*. Each of us would take a toy instrument from the handsome wooden box that had been carved by Uncle Alfred and make exuberant noises at appropriate or inappropriate moments. Or, as a family, we would sing muscial rounds and folk songs and ballads from *The Fireside Book of Folk Songs*.

Although framed as a family adventure, it was actually necessary in order to make ends meet to rent all of the rooms during the summer months both at Pilgrims Inn and in the Icehouse. Each June, we packed our belongings and moved across Devon Road into the barn as well as into a large tent on the property. The barn had probably been built at the same time as Pilgrims Inn, around 1798. There were stanchions beneath the barn for cows and stalls on the road level for horses. We moved into the apartment at the back of the barn that my parents had fixed up. We slept on simple beds in the loft.

As promised in the brochure, each morning during the Season, we served our guests a Continental breakfast of fresh homemade bread, butter and jam, fresh orange juice, coffee and tea. Ginny and I made the bread and squeezed the oranges each night before going to bed.

Early on misty summer mornings, the two of us would leave the barn and cross Devon Road to the Inn. We set up large oval metal trays on the kitchen table that was covered like a Parisian bistro with a red and white checked oilcloth. We would then carry the breakfast trays through a small gift shop to the breakfast room, the large back room where our guests sat at rose-painted wooden tables in rose-painted wooden chairs.

I made and painted a rectangular sign that we hung on hooks from the bottom of the Pilgrims Inn sign on Route 7. *Tea Served. 3:30–5:30.* Trying to attract the matinée crowd from the Berkshire Playhouse, Ginny and I made quantities of sugar tea cookies from the *Fanny Farmer Cookbook* to serve in case anyone stopped for tea.

I remember one elegant guest who came in a chauffeur-driven car. She paid her bill. We owed her 25 cents in change. We quickly polished a small silver tray, put a doily on it and a shiny 25-cent piece and delivered it to the car. The lady was astonished and insisted that we keep the change.

Because we lived two miles outside the town of Stockbridge and because the Mabies had moved away and there were no other children in the neighborhood, we five children made our own entertainment. We were allowed to go exploring by bicycle or on foot wherever and whenever we wanted. Going west across Route 7, Devon Road became Rattlesnake Mountain Road, a dirt road that wound up and over a hill past a trail that led up to what we called the Caves, past a beaver pond, and past another trail that led to a sugaring off hut. In the spring, we could watch a few locals making maple syrup. They would collect the tin buckets that had been fastened to maple trees. The buckets, overflowing with watery sap, would be emptied into flat pans over an open fire. The boiling process took hours. I loved the cold, damp air of early spring, the fire in the simple wooden lean-to in the woods, and the smell of the sap as it was reduced by the heat and turned into syrup and maple sugar candy.

I would occasionally take my small, portable camp stove and hike up to the Caves, small shelters formed by the juggling of boulders during the retreat of the Ice Age glacier that had once covered the land. On the trail, I would pick up pieces of birch bark on which I could write notes to my friends. I adored the spring flowers, the skunk cabbage, the May apples, the jack-in-the-pulpits, the violets, the Indian pipes, the trillium, the moss, and the ferns. A little later in the spring, delicate wild red columbines danced against grey granite boulders. The air was full of bird song and the smell of rich moist earth. Having arrived at the Caves, I would spread a cushion of leaves and pine branches on the floor of the largest of them, sit and make myself a cup of tea.

In the summer, we played softball and badminton. Later, my father smoothed part of the land behind the Icehouse and turned it into a croquet court. He was passionate about the game. I think he was considered at one time to be one of the best players in New England. I teased him by giving him a story that I had written and illustrated: "Mallethead: How to Keep Your Friends While Winning at Croquet."

The family often had breakfast on the fieldstone terrace under the white birch tree that towered over the house. We had picnics under the Camperdown Elm, a rare and robust specimen that grew in the courtyard. Years later when we sold the Inn, the new owner, trying to destroy some bushes that grew close to the tree, doused the area with Round-Up and killed the tree. I was shocked by his random, thoughtless use of dangerous chemicals.

I loved climbing trees, especially the tall Norwegian pine behind Pilgrims Inn. I remember taking a small ax and a saw and cutting a path through the branches and twigs to the treetop. A storm had broken off the top of the pine and left a small flat stump. Sometimes I would take a book to the top of the tree, sit and read and survey the countryside.

The Prince and Princess Sapieha were White Russian artists who had fled Russia and found sanctuary in the Berkshires. They lived in a large white clapboard house at the end of the long driveway that passed to the left of the barn. If they saw me clambering about in the huge maple tree beside Devon Road, they would shout, "Come down. Come down. You are too beautiful to die." They asked if they could paint my portrait. I would walk down the driveway to their house to pose for them, intrigued by the easels and brushes and oil paints and by their accents. I still have a wooden sewing box that they gave me. It is turquoise with painted scenes from the story of Hansel and Gretel.

Apparently, our little corner of the Berkshires attracted royalty. I recently learned that Queen Wilhelmina of the Netherlands, a leader of the Dutch Resistance during WWII, spent the summer of 1942 with her daughter Juliana and her granddaughter Beatrix in a house at the east end of Devon Road. The Germans occupied the Netherlands at the time, and, as a courtesy to the Queen, President Franklin D. Roosevelt not only arranged her stay but visited her several times during the summer.

In the fall, we children played our own version of war, pelting each other with brown, glossy horse chestnuts that had fallen from the massive horse chestnut tree that grew next to the front porch of Pilgrims Inn. We always had a bonfire with the brilliant maple leaves that we had raked into an enormous pile. You didn't have to have a fire permit in those days. The marshes and meadows were now full of cattails and milkweed, Joe Pye weed, purple asters, goldenrod, and Queen Anne's Lace. There were square dances in the town hall in West Stockbridge. *Swing your partner, round and round, now dosey doe.*

One of our favorite activities in the summer and fall was to climb past huge granite boulders to the top of Monument Mountain, a literary landmark in the Berkshires. On August 5, 1850, Herman Melville, Nathaniel Hawthorne and Oliver Wendell Holmes took a bottle of champagne to the summit and read a poem that told of the lovesick Mohican maiden who, dressed in her finest jewelry and with flowers woven into her hair, had thrown herself off the mountain. Because of tribal custom, she had been forbidden to marry the warrior cousin whom she loved. Everyone in the Berkshires could recite that tale and show you the spot from which she had jumped to her death and the rock cairn below that marked her burial spot.

> *"There was a maid, the fairest of Indian maids, bright-eyed with wealth of raven tresses, a light form, and a gay heart. About her cabin door the wide old woods resounded with her song and fairy laughter of the summer day . . .*
>
> *"But when the sun grew low and the hill shadows long, she threw herself from the steep rock and perished . . ."*
>
> —WILLIAM CULLEN BRYANT
> *Monument Mountain* (1815)

I felt so sorry for her. I wondered if her lover was equally distraught and tried to kill himself, too. Was this a Romeo and Juliet story?

In the winter, we had snowball fights and went sledding and ice skating. Once, playing ice hockey on a bumpy frozen local pond, I tripped while chasing the puck and drove the metal blade on the back of my figure skate under my right kneecap. The cut was deep and required a number of stitches, but there was no lasting harm. Thinking about Peter Berle, the strong, handsome boy who had rescued me and carried me off the ice, helped deaden the pain.

During cold evenings in front of the fire in the front room of Pilgrims Inn, we drank hot chocolate and played Parcheesi or Scrabble or put together the wooden jig-saw puzzles with their dark-toned English literary and pub scenes that had belonged to the Ripley family.

I remember one winter party when I was sixteen or seventeen. We had invited friends to a holiday dance in the ballroom, the spacious room at the back of Pilgrims Inn that also served as the breakfast room during the summer. We decorated the ballroom with red candles and with the evergreen boughs that we had collected in the woods during the day. We had a record player by then and played music for dancing, mostly waltzes and foxtrots.

It was a great party. Everyone was in high spirits and there was much laughter from the moment the guests came in from the cold, brushing snow from their coats. I remember Susan and Kai Erikson were there, the children of Joan and Erik Erikson, the psychologist and author of the seminal *Childhood and Society* (1950) and *Identity: Youth and Crisis* (1968). Much later, when we lived in Cambridge, I would see the Eriksons walking hand-in-hand along the Charles River. Theirs seemed like a remarkable marriage, a real partnership. To this day Joan Erikson, with her intelligence, sensitivity, and obvious strength of character and independence, remains one of the women I most admire.

We had a number of fascinating guests each summer who became friends and who returned to Pilgrims Inn every year. I think they liked the homey atmosphere and the cheerful young girls who made bread and cookies, sewed their own aprons, and created their own fun.

My mother also hired a young woman to help each summer. One year, she hired Gulbun from Turkey. Gulbun was quite shocked at the casual way that my father was greeted when he came home from his workday at the bank. She said that in her country, men were pampered and coddled, especially after a day at work. She taught us to treat our father with more overt respect and care. We began to welcome him with a glass of water when he came home from work and encouraged him to sit down and tell us about his day. We called this the "Turkish Treatment."

Another year she hired Marilyn De Beuss, the daughter of the then Dutch Ambassador to the United States. She came for the Boston Symphony Orchestra but mostly for Charles Munch, the French conductor. She may have had an introduction from her father, but whether or not that was the case, she made a connection with Charles Munch. Maybe it was because she sat in the front row during all of the Tanglewood concerts when he was conducting.

Late one summer night, my sisters and I stayed up in the barn waiting for Marilyn to return from the final performance of the season. It must have been in 1958 on the night before the orchestra left on its first overseas tour. It was well after midnight and Marilyn had not yet appeared. Suddenly a fancy black car drove up and parked in front of the barn. It stayed there for a few minutes, then the car door slammed, the latch on the barn door clicked open and Marilyn came in, looking tousled and radiant. She said that after the final concert, Munch had offered to drive her home. They spent some time lying in a meadow looking at the stars, she said. Before he left, he gave her the baton that he had used that summer during the Tanglewood season. She waved it exultantly as she came into the barn. We were spell-bound. Lying in a meadow and looking at the stars? The season's baton?

The Stockbridge Plain School on Main Street in Stockbridge was a public school with classrooms for students from the first through the eighth grade. Williams High School (grades 9–12) was located in the same building. I attended the school for the last few months of the fifth grade through the tenth grade before being sent away to boarding school. There was no middle school.

I took the yellow school bus to and from school every day. On some icy winter mornings, waiting beside Route 7 for the school bus, the skin on my legs was rubbed raw by the rough edges of my rubber boots. Although the school was only two miles from our home, it was a forty-minute bus ride each way. For some reason, we always went the long way past Tanglewood. The bus driver, Mr. Green, was fat, chewed on cigars, and had a large and ugly growth of some sort behind his left ear.

I had an excellent teacher, Miss Farrell, organized and creative, in the sixth grade; an incompetent teacher, Miss Wolf, disorganized and dull, in the seventh; and the grade school principal, Mr. Blair, in the eighth grade. Mr. Blair was a heavyset older man and a disciplinarian. I didn't like or trust him. He seemed more interested in teasing the young girls in our class about their developing breasts than in being a creative teacher. His behavior would not be tolerated in today's world where young girls have been taught to report such inappropriate behavior to their parents or to school officials.

Once I talked back to him. He punished me by making me memorize the Gettysburg Address, then making me recite it three times in front of the class. "*. . . that government by the people, for the people and of the people shall not perish from this earth . . .*" I was frustrated and talked back to him again, "Do you want me to recite it backwards?" It's a wonder that I wasn't expelled. I clearly didn't tolerate instructions from adults whom I did not respect.

For a similar disrespectful offense, Miss Wolf in the seventh grade made me stay after school, copy twenty times and memorize Rudyard Kipling's poem, "If." "*If you can keep your head when all about you are losing theirs and blaming it on you . . . .*" A useful poem, full of life lessons, except that it was dedicated to boys, not girls. If you followed the advice in the poem, "*. . . you'll be a man, my son.*"

Mr. Clarke was my Latin teacher in the ninth grade, the first year at Williams High School. Unsmiling and tough, he accused me once of copying my Latin homework from someone else. I was extremely upset. The homework was my own. I told my mother who marched immediately to the school and confronted Mr. Clarke, telling him that he was never again to accuse me of lying. We had certain unbreakable rules and standards in our family and telling the truth was one of them. I appreciated my mother's belief in me and her loyalty.

The playground was behind the school building. During recess, we climbed on huge boulders. When the earth was damp, we dug shallow holes in the soil and played marbles. I think that we called the big marbles "boulders." We played hopscotch and thought up challenging songs and exercises for jumping rope. There was a wooden seesaw in the playground that you could adjust so that the person on the other end popped up into the air screaming with fear. I think that seesaws have been banned from playgrounds today, considered too dangerous.

Girls, in those days, at least in the public Stockbridge Plain School, did not play sports. They could be cheerleaders, but only boys could play on the basketball and baseball teams or take courses in carpentry. In our high school, there were homemaking courses for the girls where they could learn to cook and sew. It seemed strange to me, even then in the 1950s, that parents and schools seemed to dedicate most of their resources to educating and promoting boys. I didn't actively question this, however. I just accepted it. It was part of the culture of the time.

GOAL! It is now June 2019. As I write, I am thrilled as I watch on television strong, confident young women from all over the world competing in the Women's World Cup Soccer Finals. How far female athletes have come in the past decades, from being limited to cheerleading to being able to compete at the highest level in their chosen sports.

Often after school, we students from the Stockbridge Plain School would wander down Main Street to the drugstore. It was a favorite hangout with counter stools that spun around and a few booths where you could sit with friends. With your allowance money, you could order a frappe or ginger ale with a scoop of ice cream. Norman Rockwell painted the drugstore scene. It was one of his most famous paintings, later made into posters and puzzles.

Norman Rockwell's studio was on the second floor of a building opposite the drugstore. It had a large picture window overlooking Main Street. If Rockwell saw someone who might be a good model for one of his paintings, he would send an aide to the drugstore to ask if that person might be willing to sit for him. Everyone in town knew and loved Norman Rockwell and his wife, Molly Punderson, so this request was not considered unusual or peculiar.

When I was fourteen, he called me up to his studio and took a number of photographs, headshots, that he used to paint my profile for an advertisement in *The Saturday Evening Post.* I found the advertisement a number of years later in a large book of his works at the Norman Rockwell Museum in Stockbridge. Several summers ago, on what the Rockwell Museum calls Models Day, I was invited along with other models to sit at a table with that painting in front of me. Members of the public passed by, glancing first at the youthful figures in the paintings, then looking up to see how the models had aged.

The high school students occasionally held dances in the gym. They were always heavily chaperoned by parents. Someone played records. There wasn't much dancing. The boys usually stood talking and kidding each other on one side of the gym while the equally self-conscious girls gossiped and giggled on the other. As a sophomore, I was crowned queen at the annual spring dance. I also attended two Christmas Cotillions in Pittsfield where each girl was given a dance card to be filled out, she hoped, by some of the young men ogling the girls from the other side of the room.

How well I remember dressing for a high school dance in a yellow strapless chiffon dress over a starched lace petticoat that I had made. Hurrying back to the house to get something that I had forgotten, I tripped and fell into a muddy puddle in full view of my parents and my young date eager to present me with a corsage. I think that I had also stuffed the top of the dress with white bobby socks that popped out when I fell.

Even though the United States and Russia had been allies in the fight against Nazi Germany in World War II, they became suspicious of each other shortly after the war ended. Russia was a Marxist-Leninist Communist state under the dictator Stalin. The United States was a constitutional democracy. Both countries had nuclear weapons. We were taught in school about the Cold War and to fear the Russians and their nuclear weapons. We thought about bomb shelters and how we would provision them. The possibility of nuclear war was a deep fear.

I distinctly remember walking along Devon Road, the dirt road outside our house and wondering whether my family should build a bomb shelter and if we did, what we should put in it. I remember worrying about what would happen, if there were a nuclear war, to the little creatures that have no voice, the birds and bees and butterflies and little rabbits. That thought troubled me then. It troubles me still.

In early June of 1954, I was in Washington, D.C. visiting Aunt H. Everyone was watching the McCarthy hearings on television or listening to the hearings on the radio.

Joseph McCarthy, a Republican senator from Wisconsin, had gripped and terrified the country for two years. On television, playing on Cold War fears but without evidence, he accused people of being Communist sympathizers (Reds) and traitors. He ruined the lives of many writers, actors, teachers and government employees. He claimed that Communists had infiltrated the State Department and the CIA. He required people to take loyalty oaths.

On June 9, 1954 Senator McCarthy accused Joseph Welch who was representing the Army of being a complicit Communist, stating that one of his young associates was a Red. There was a pause. Silence. Then Joseph Welch said, "Have you no sense of decency, sir, at long last? Have you no sense of decency?" Those simple words spoken by a thoughtful man of integrity somehow struck home. The hearings ended, just like that. The nation realized that it had been captivated by a dangerous, cruel, power-hungry huckster and demagogue. I was fifteen at the time. The thought that common decency expressed in simple words could win over cruel demagoguery made a great impression on me. In my opinion, our nation today is in thrall to a hate-and-fear-spewing conman, President Donald Trump. I only hope that, like Senator McCarthy, he will soon be revealed to be a dangerous fraud and removed from the presidency.

The Town of Stockbridge was settled in 1734 by English missionaries who hoped to convert the Mohican Indians —later called the Stockbridge Indians—from their heathen practices to Christianity. When we moved to Stockbridge in 1950, the population was about 2,000. Tom Carey in his horse and buggy still carried the mail every morning from the train station to the post office. The phone service was primitive. When you wanted to make a call, you picked up the telephone from its cradle on the table. A local operator, quite likely someone from town whom you knew, would ask for the name of the party you wanted to reach. She would place the call for you. As everyone in town was on a party line, you would often find yourself eavesdropping on other conversations. There were red boxy phone booths on the sidewalks. If you wanted to make a call while in town, you put a nickel or a dime in the coin slot and dialed your number with a rotary dial.

The marvel of the smart phone didn't exist at that time, even in people's wildest imaginations or fantasies. No one could envision that a time would come when a hand-held phone would contain more information than a million encyclopedias or that a *Cloud* would be filled, not with rain or hail or snow, but with data.

I sometimes wonder what will surprise us in the future. We are already beginning to imagine that roads might soon be covered with driverless cars and that human hands might be replaced with clever robotic fingers. In the new field of Artificial Intelligence (AI), there is talk of AI tools that will be able to track thought and perhaps someday, download a person's knowledge and memories to preserve for posterity. Maybe someday, written autobiographies like this one will be obsolete. Children and grandchildren might be able to learn a life-story with its thoughts and ideas, even its memories, from a chip that they remove from their grandparent's brain. A chilling thought. But possible?

Norman Rockwell's famous painting, *Main Street, Stockbridge at Christmas*, shows the Red Lion Inn, decorated for the holidays. The Inn was built in 1773, just before the Revolutionary War. It is still running, in continuous operation for almost 250 years. In addition to the Stockbridge Plain School and the Red Lion Inn, Main Street in Stockbridge is known for other interesting and distinguished buildings. There is the Stockbridge Public Library and Museum, the historic Mission House, the Austen Riggs Center, a psychiatric treatment center where Dr. Erik Erikson practiced, and Saint Paul's Episcopal Church.

Designed by Charles McKim, the same architect who designed the Boston Public Library and the Morgan Library in New York City, Saint Paul's is a stunning stone, Norman-style church with exquisite stained glass windows, wood carvings, and a high relief on the wall below the choir stall, a replica of a frieze by Luca della Robbia. To ring the church bells, one would grab a heavy rope located just inside the side entrance to the church and pull down hard. If the bell ringer was light-weight, he or she would ride the rope right up to the ceiling. That was so much fun that sometimes the magnificent pealing went on and on, surprising and maybe alarming the townsfolk. On the porch just outside the entrance stands a small, elegant, bronze winged figure called *The Spirit of Life*. It was sculpted by Daniel Chester French, a resident of Stockbridge and famous for his sculpture of the seated Abraham Lincoln in the Lincoln Memorial in Washington, DC.

For a number of years, we, at least my mother and her three daughters, attended Saint Paul's on Sundays. During the long and, to me, boring sermons, I would study the figures on the stained glass windows and try to figure out the story. I liked singing hymns, especially martial ones like "Onward, Christian Soldiers." I was willing to go to church, as it was an opportunity to meet people and see my friends. I especially liked the doughnuts and cider offered in the parish house after the service.

In my early teenage years, as I didn't know anything about sex or what a virgin was, I never understood or thought much about the references the minister made to the Immaculate Conception or to the Virgin Birth. I couldn't understand the concept of a Resurrection, either, as I thought that when one was dead, one was dead. I had buried small dead animals, rabbits, little birds, even a skunk, and they hadn't come back to life. Why should humans be any different? And I thought the concept of the Trinity was strange. I didn't think that it possible that God had a son who was also a ghost. And a holy one at that.

In any case, I intoned the Apostles Creed just like everyone else. I knelt on the prayer stools for the prayers. And I took Communion, although I didn't know what it signified to partake of Christ's Body and drink His Blood. I thought that everyone in the congregation, myself included, was putting on an act trying to look sincere. When I walked down the main aisle from the Communion rail back to my seat in the pew, I tried to appear suitably reverent, eyes downcast, hands clasped in front of me. It was an effort, as I really wanted to look for certain boys in the congregation. And I wanted them to look at me.

Although I didn't like being preached at during the Sunday sermons, I did love certain special occasions at St. Paul's Church. The midnight Christmas Eve service was beautiful with tall tapers and evergreen boughs attached to the end of each pew. I appreciated the organ's deep tones and sang with gusto most of the verses of the Christmas carols. At midnight, the congregation chorused

"Joy to the World" and filed out of the church passing a group of bell ringers playing handbells on the church steps.

Ignoring the Sunday sermons, I would gaze instead at the sunlight filtering through the stained glass windows. Sometimes, to pass the time, I would read the Psalms at the back of the Book of Common Prayer. I memorized some of them. I remember to this day the Benediction spoken by the minister at the end of each worship service:

> *"May the Lord bless you and keep you. May the Lord make His face to shine upon you and be gracious unto you. May the Lord lift up the Light of His countenance upon you and bring you peace, this day and forevermore. Amen."*

Walking down Main Street in Stockbridge after school to visit the library or the drugstore, I once met another ninth grader who went to the Catholic Church a block away. I asked him what he was learning there. He intoned a short answer, as if he had memorized the message: "One flock, one Shepherd." I remember picturing the sheep and thinking that his mind at the Catholic Church was being filled with different visuals than mine just a block away at the Episcopal Church. Then he mentioned that everyone was born in sin. After failing to understand that, I nevertheless began to wonder: did he have the right message, the one that would take you to heaven, or did I? I still thought that there might be a heaven, although when I looked up at the sky, I couldn't figure out where it might be or why no one had ever come back and told their friends about it.

At the western end of Main Street, the road turns sharply to the right, onto Route 102. A few blocks along this road on the right is the entrance to the historic Stockbridge Cemetery. The ashes of George and Ruth Ripley, my father and mother, are buried there in a plot that looks across a tranquil field and up the hill to Naumkeg, one of the historic Berkshire Cottages.

When my father died, my brothers George and Franklin dragged a handsome pyramidal stone down from Monument Mountain. It serves as a headstone for the plot. Engraved on the front is: *In Tenderness and Trust.* On the back are engraved the words: *Light, Beauty, Grace,* and *Love.* I hope that my ashes will join theirs in that spot someday.

My parents sent me away to boarding school at the age of fifteen because they wanted to challenge me academically. My mother and father wanted all of their children to have a liberal arts college education, and they could see that very few students, girls or boys, went to liberal arts colleges from Williams High School in Stockbridge.

It is interesting to note that, typical of girls growing up in the 1940's and 1950s, I had never been encouraged to reach for the stars professionally, either by my parents or by my teachers. I was never told that with a dream and a will, I could be anything I wanted to be. Decades passed before I met a female doctor, lawyer, architect, pastor, entrepreneur, or school principal, to say nothing of a female astronaut. I never wondered about that or questioned it. I assumed that after college I would follow in my mother's footsteps. I would marry and raise a family. I assumed that men were entitled to hold all of the important, influential, and interesting positions in society. After all, stories about men dominated the political, sports, business, arts, and even the obituary sections of newspapers. In bookstores and libraries, it was hard to find biographies of talented, adventurous, or successful women. With few exceptions, like the Nancy Drew mystery stories I loved, even children's books featured the dreams, the quests, the adventures, and the achievements of young boys. In addition, despite the fact that I knew that Aunt H was living independently, the thought that I should or could prepare to earn my own living never occurred to me or apparently to my parents.

I was sent to an Episcopal boarding school called Saint Mary's-in-the-Mountains in Littleton, New Hampshire. The school was also known as Saint Mags-in-the-Crags, Saint Mary's, or just SMS. There were eighty students in the four high school classes, twenty girls to a class. Why did my parents send me to such a small girls' school in a remote corner of northern New Hampshire? I can only think that, in addition to giving me a better education, they wanted to get me away from boys. Boys in Stockbridge had begun to show an interest in me, and I was interested in them. I know that my parents worried when older boys took me driving in their cars. Far away in Littleton, New Hampshire, I would be safe. There was not a boy to be found within one hundred miles.

My parents had sent my older sister Ginny to the National Cathedral School in Washington, D.C. Not only was Saint Albans, the brother school, nearby, Washington had a rich cultural environment. Aunt H lived there as well and could educate Ginny about the political world. Later, my parents sent my sister Anne to Abbot Academy in Andover, a boarding school for girls across the street from my grandparents' home. It was a school with a rich academic and cultural tradition. Boys were just up the hill at Phillips Andover. I was quite envious of both of my sisters.

Ginny and I attended our schools on scholarships. I think that the Episcopal Church helped with the expenses of both Saint

Mary's and the National Cathedral School. So perhaps spending Sunday mornings at church had been worthwhile.

Miss Jenks was the headmistress of Saint Mary's. She was a rigid, joyless spinster who ran the school with a tight hand. Study halls were completely silent and some meals as well. Good table manners were stressed. Bad ones received a reprimand.

I liked most of my classes at SMS, especially my class in art history taught by an Englishman, Hamish MacEwan. I did my research on index cards and wrote my papers in longhand. I also liked Madame Belinska's class in elocution and declamation where we were forced to enunciate every microscopic syllable of a Wordsworth poem. *"I wandered lonely as a cloud that floats on high o'er vales and hills, when all at once I saw a crowd, a host of golden daffodils . . ."* I liked the way we had to pause before emphasizing "**host**" using a higher and stronger voice.

Before my senior year, my parents gave me a small travel typewriter in a tan vinyl case. I started learning to type making carbon copies of my papers. My typewriter became my most prized possession.

In early November of 1956, as editor of the school newspaper, I was asked to give a short talk at a special school meeting. In late October, Russian Communists had rolled their tanks into Budapest, Hungary ignoring the townsfolk who had met them and tried to deter them, as I remember, by offering bouquets of flowers to the soldiers. The soldiers paid no attention. Many civilians were killed. The Hungarian uprising against Soviet rule was crushed. It was considered to be the first attack on the so-called Iron Curtain, the symbol of the Cold War between Communist Russia and the West. In my speech, I spoke about the need to be vigilant and brave in the fight against tyranny.

I mention this uprising because a year or so later one of the revolutionaries about whom I had spoken found his way to the Berkshires, to Pilgrims Inn and to the barn. He was a sculptor. I think his name was George. He knocked on the door of Pilgrims Inn and asked whether he could live in the barn and sculpt in exchange for doing repairs to the barn. Another artist for the commune. Another interesting person. My mother, intrigued, agreed.

We had no idea what he was sculpting until several years later when he moved away. When we went into his section of the barn, we found about twenty full-sized nude figures of women carved out of white limestone, all doing mundane things like curling their hair or putting on lipstick. The models, we learned later, had been the good women of Stockbridge.

We also found that our Hungarian revolutionary had done no work to maintain the barn. His section of the barn was a disaster. There was no question but that we had to clean it up. This included disposing of the limestone ladies. But what could we to do with them? I remembered that there was a deep limestone quarry in Lee, the neighboring town. Maybe we could put them there. Ashes to ashes, dust to dust, why not limestone to limestone?

We loaded the ladies into the back of a pick-up truck and drove them to the quarry. Without guilt or remorse, we eased them into the water one by one. Perhaps someday, an archaeologist in a wet suit will dive to the bottom of the quarry and think that he has discovered an ancient and mysterious civilization, one that preceded by millennia the local Mohican tribe. He will write his doctoral thesis on his astonishing find.

My overwhelming memory, however, of the two school years that I spent at Saint Mary's is one of feeling extraordinarily lonely and isolated. It didn't help that during my first year, I had to share a small room and bath with five other girls. I was deeply homesick for my family and for the stimulating life at Pilgrims Inn. I missed the town of Stockbridge so much that my mother went around town with pre-addressed and stamped postcards asking the postman, the man behind the counter at the drugstore, and various merchants who knew me to write to me with the news of the town.

I was sixteen and seventeen years old during those years and so full of longing that I remember on several cloudy and windy days walking to the top of a hill a little distance from the school. There, I would sing at the top of my lungs:

> *"Once on a high and windy hill, in the morning mist, two lovers kissed, and the world stood still. Then your fingers touched my silent heart and taught it how to sing. Yes, true love's a many-splendored thing."*

The romantic film, *Love is a Many-Splendored Thing,* had just been released. The thought of being able to make a silent heart sing made me swoon.

It helped lift my spirits to go back to Pilgrims Inn during school breaks. Because most of my siblings were away either at school or college, the rooms of the Inn were now filled by actors, sculptors, poets and musicians. From what I have read, communes established during the 1960s in the United States seem to have been characterized by sex, drugs, and rock-and-roll. This was not the case in the 1950s at Pilgrims Inn. The people whom I met who lived there were creative, highly educated individuals who respected one another and enjoyed one another's company.

The kitchen table with its red and white checked oilcloth

covering was still the heart of the Inn. Everyone gathered there for morning coffee and afternoon tea. I remember the Hungarian sculptor who wandered in from the barn. I remember studying him and wondering how he had escaped during the revolution. Gabriella Sedgewick, the poet, came in from the little cabin that my brother Franklin had built on the property. One morning, she showed everyone her collection of stunning photographs of black-figured Greek vases. Paula Obermeier from France and her musical family might bring a bowl of wheat berries for everyone to try. On some early misty summer mornings, Romeo from Shakespeare & Company would bring to the table a bowl of raspberries that he and I had just picked in the raspberry patch in the meadow.

For about a decade, even after their five children had left home for boarding schools and colleges and after my mother and father had returned to live in the Icehouse, they continued to fill Pilgrims Inn's ten bedrooms with actors, musicians, sculptors, artists and poets and writers. My mother's dream of creating a fellowship of artists and thinkers had come true.

Sending me away to Saint Mary's had accomplished my parents' goals. It kept me completely away from boys. And it gave me enough academic credibility that when I applied to Wellesley, Smith, and Wheaton Colleges, I was accepted at all three, all women's colleges. In 1957, none of the men's Ivy League colleges accepted women. I would enter college the following September. There was no alternative at that time, such as taking a Gap Year. If you planned to go to college, you would enter in the fall immediately after high school.

I spent the summer between high school and college in Ely, Vermont working as a junior counselor at Aloha Hive, a camp for girls where both my mother and Aunt H had spent happy times. Mine was not a happy time, however. It seems that I must have spent my extra hours eating seconds and thirds of a sugary, slurpy, chocolate concoction called Mississippi Mud. I arrived at the camp a slim girl weighing 118 pounds. I left thirty pounds heavier after two months of gorging. When my mother saw me, she was appalled. I was, too. I was embarrassed that I had to wear my mother's clothes. When she found out that it was the camp's mission to see how many pounds each camper could gain during her stay, she was furious. She wrote letters to the camp directors demanding that they eliminate that policy.

I ate lightly for what remained of the summer, then started packing for the trip east over the newly completed Massachusetts Turnpike. When I entered Wellesley College in the fall of 1957, I carried with me a copy of *A Treasury of the Theater* (Scribner's Sons, 1957), my prize for winning the English award at my graduation from Saint Mary's in-the-Mountains.

I was seventeen years old.

Chapter Four

Choices

Wellesley College and Marriage (1957–1960)

I chose Wellesley College for two reasons: the natural beauty of the campus and the fact that my sister Ginny would be living on campus as a sophomore. In 1957, the all-inclusive cost for tuition, room and board at Wellesley was $1,900. To help cover personal expenses, I signed up for a part-time job in the Well, a snack bar in the basement of Tower Court. At the start of my freshman year, my parents helped me arrange my room on the second floor of Shafer Hall, one of the dorms in the Quadrangle. My biggest treasure was a soft, white, hand-woven woolen blanket, a special gift to me from my mother.

My freshman roommate in Shafer Hall was thin, wiry, mischievous, and interested only in smoking cigarettes illegally and playing card games on the floor of our room. She planned to major in math. Walking back to the dorm one afternoon in the winter, I saw five hook and ladder fire trucks from the Town of Wellesley Fire Department below the window of our room. I dashed upstairs to find everything in the room, including my precious blanket, coated with a putrid, brownish, oily, chemical substance. My roommate, wanting to find out if the sprinkler system worked, had climbed up onto the bureau, then had reached up and using pliers had activated the sprinkler system on the ceiling. Foul-smelling sludge that I was sure had been in the system for generations flooded the room. I was devastated.

My roommate was sent to live in another dorm. I spent several months living alone in an unfurnished attic space in the dorm. Eventually, I was allowed to return to my room which had been cleaned, deodorized, and turned into a single.

I felt overwhelmed academically during my freshman year. Even after two years of college prep at Saint Mary's, I did not feel ready for college work. It was hard for me to turn out the papers required in every class. Although I had taken basic English classes, I hadn't been taught the differences between expository, creative or reportorial writing, or the subtle ways meaning can be altered or enhanced with similes and metaphors.

I took voluminous notes by hand in each class that I later transferred to index cards. Laboriously making carbon copies of everything, I wrote papers on my prized typewriter. I was envious of the girls who not only seemed to be unfazed by the written assignments but who appeared confident and articulate when speaking in class. They also seemed to know how to manage their time, balancing academics and extracurricular activities.

Also, I wasn't used to abstract thinking. I had absolutely no idea, for example, what the freshman philosophy professor was talking about when we studied the shadows in Plato's Cave. Furthermore, I couldn't fathom why learning about those shadows could be important. I preferred to wander the beautiful campus and study the shadows caused by shafts of sunlight and moonlight on Lake Waban.

In general, at that time, the choices for female students even at the finest women's colleges were limited. It was assumed that a graduate could aspire to become a teacher, a nurse, a secretary, a social worker, a librarian, maybe a scholar or, most likely, a wife and mother married to a man who would provide for and protect her and their family. The last option was the life plan that Wellesley implicitly and society in general supported. It was rare that a young woman might have dreams beyond those acceptable aspirations.

It is interesting to note that in the late 1950s, no women were accepted for graduate programs at the Harvard Business School (HBS) and only a few at the Harvard Law and Medical Schools. Participating in a service project after finishing college was not an alternative, the way it is today for thousands of students. For example, the Peace Corps, an exceptional new opportunity for service and personal growth, was founded in 1961, the year my college class graduated. Occasionally, I was teased that we Wellesley *girls*, not *women*, were studying for a Mrs, not a BA, a Bachelor of Arts. I didn't question this expectation. It was part of the culture of the time. Men had professional lives in order to provide a home for their wives and children.

The movie *Mona Lisa Smile,* starring Julia Roberts, released in 2003 and filmed on the Wellesley College campus, supports that cultural reality of the 1950s. I identify with that film, in part because the action takes place in the art history department. The graduating students at that time were most proud of their engagement rings.

I wasn't musing about these things, however, on April 9, 1958, a beautiful spring afternoon in my freshman year. I had been playing tennis and was walking back to Shafer Hall. My room was on the second floor directly above the back door that was kept locked. If I could find someone to unlock the back door, I would not have to walk to the front entrance at the far end of the building, a fair distance away.

I saw my Dutch friend Talitha Boone sitting in the window of her room next to the back door. She was soaking up the sun and talking with someone who was standing in the bushes. I went up the steps to the landing and asked her if she would be kind enough to unlock the back door for me so that I could more easily reach my room.

She agreed and left her perch on the windowsill. I looked to my right to see who was in the bushes. Standing there was a young handsome man with a warm, friendly smile and bright blue eyes.

For both of us, it was, as the French say, a *coup de foudre,* a thunderbolt, and love at first sight. "Do you play tennis?" he asked. My tennis racket was a dead give-away.

"Yes," I answered, "Do you?" Then for some reason, I became bold. I think that it was his eyes and his smile. "Would you like to play? I can run upstairs and get another racket."

That was it. On that day in April sixty-two years ago, the smiling, blue-eyed young man and I connected like two magnets. Off we went to play tennis. I learned that his name was Ralph Sorenson, better known as Bud, and that he was studying for a master's degree at HBS. We made plans to get together again soon.

The following week we attended Wellesley Night at the Boston Pops at Symphony Hall. When Bud spontaneously bought a pitcher of sangria for the next table, I was smitten. *Not only is he smart and comfortable and exciting to be with*, I thought to myself, *he is also generous and kind! And those blue eyes*!

In the following weeks, we picnicked on Crane's Beach on the North Shore and went to Ola's, a tiny Norwegian restaurant in

Boston where we talked about our common Norwegian ancestry. I fell in love. Bud had made my silent heart sing. Apparently his heart was singing, too.

In the summer, Bud drove to Stockbridge to visit Pilgrims Inn and meet my family. For some reason, wanting to make a good first impression, I spent the morning on a ladder washing a rust streak off the side of the house! Then, overwhelmed by confusing thoughts, I went off to volunteer at the music festival at Tanglewood, making sure that I would not be at home when he arrived. Perhaps I wanted to challenge Bud, to see if he could meet and handle my unconventional family on his own. He passed my test with flying colors. Everyone loved him.

During my sophomore and junior years at Wellesley, I lived in Munger Hall where I made many life-long friends including Connie, Debby C., Debby S., Janet, Jackie, JoAnne, Judy, Martha Mel, Phoebe Ann, Sarah, Sigrid, and Willinda. This special group has traveled each year for the past few decades to some fascinating place in this country or abroad. I treasure these friendships.

In spite of the strict parietal rules like evening curfews, no men in the dorm, and the obligatory written permission from a parent in order to leave the campus for an overnight, Bud and I dated during my sophomore year while he finished his MBA (Master of Business of Administration). After graduation, he planned to work as a research associate at IMEDE (*L'Institute pour L'Etude des Methodes de Direction de L'Entreprise*), an international school of management established by faculty members from HBS and located on the shore of Lake Geneva in Lausanne, Switzerland.

My sister Ginny and I learned during my sophomore year that an Italian Renaissance professor, Curtis Shell, and a professor of Biblical History, Charles Hall, were taking a small group of Wellesley students that summer to Italy for three months to study art. In a generous gesture, Aunt H gave each of us the gift of the trip. Bud arranged to go to Europe with our group on the *Arkadia,* a shabby, rusty Greek ocean liner.

We stayed in Paris for a few days, then Bud left for Lausanne and our group traveled to Florence. Bud and I agreed that, if possible, I should spend a few days visiting him in Lausanne. I did, soon afterwards, traveling by train through the dark Simplon Tunnel under Mont Blanc, the highest mountain in Europe.

Bud and I spent a magical weekend hiking in the Valais, the valley of the Rhone River. We climbed to a mountain lake, le Lac de Tanay, and picnicked in an alpine meadow on strawberries, cheese, bread and wine. We were overjoyed to be together in this beautiful meadow embroidered with buttercups, gentians and wild rhododendron. We were in love.

Bud's tiny studio apartment in Lausanne was directly above the train tracks of the main train station. Trains pulled in and out all day and all night. The air was polluted and noisy. When night came, there was no question in my mind about sleeping arrangements. I put Bud out on the balcony above the train tracks, went inside and closed and locked the balcony door. Then, holding a thick woven strap, I lowered the heavy wooden, louvered blind that covered the balcony door and windows. Absolutely no trespassing!

It was 1959, a year or so before the FDA approved the Pill for contraceptive use. It was fourteen years before the Supreme Court legalized abortion in *Roe v. Wade.* (1973). Unlike today when having sexual relationships before marriage is culturally accepted, pre-marital sex in the 1950s was considered taboo. My mother had never talked about sex, except to warn her three daughters that having sex before marriage had potentially dangerous consequences, especially for girls. It wasn't a question of whether having sex was right or wrong. For my parents, sex just wasn't as interesting a topic as the many other aspects of life we could discuss. This approach to sex and sex education was not uncommon at that time or in the semi-Victorian culture of the Eastern seaboard.

Bud's warmth, kindness, intelligence, curiosity, energy, sense of humor, and eagerness and enthusiasm for life were what I treasured. Our friendship prospered. There were long mountain hikes, explorations of the city and countryside, and wonderful conversations over candlelit dinners. I think that intuitively I felt that having sex before marriage would have complicated and challenged a wonderful, developing relationship. At the train station, before my return to Florence, we promised to write during the coming year. I think we both knew, or at least sensed at that time, that our relationship might flower into something more permanent.

Under the tutelage of our professors, Ginny and I spent our Italian summer in museums and grottos, in Romanesque chapels and Gothic cathedrals. In Florence in the Ufizzi, we studied the early Duccios and Giottos and Botticelli's *Primavera* and *The Birth of Venus*. We contemplated Massaccio's *Expulsion from the Garden of Eden*, Michelangelo's *David* and the exquisite silver work of Benvenuto Cellini. From Naples, we visited Pompeii and Herculaneum. In Ravenna, we were awestruck by the breathtaking Byzantine mosaics. That summer trip sealed my decision to major in Art History at Wellesley. My mind was alive with new ideas. At some point in this journey, I wrote to Bud:

> I wish I could tell you how this trip has affected me in my feelings toward people, culture, etc. An attitude is

> so intangible. There have been a few times, once in Florence in the Brancacci Chapel and in Rome in the Vatican Museum, when I have felt completely fired by the intellect, so to speak. I can understand that for earnest art historians like Professor Shell, art history could become a driving passion. To understand a style, to be able to trace the hand of one artist, to recognize a work of real value among works of lesser quality must be a real thrill. I've found what a deep interest in something gives to a person—a Direction!

After leaving our Wellesley group in August, Bud met Ginny and me for a rendez-vous in Venice and drove us in his new Volkswagen Bug to Vienna. He then returned to Lausanne, while Ginny and I traveled to Sweden to visit Gunnar Engellau, a family friend. We spent time with him and his family on his island off the south-west coast and in his home in Goteborg. Ginny went on to Norway where she made a sudden decision to spend the school year in Oslo, studying Norwegian and working for a family as an *au pair*. I, in turn, sailed west across the Atlantic with the Wellesley group and a huge, mysterious box.

My mother had always yearned to go to Paris. When Ginny and I tried to think of a gift to take to our mother, it was clear. What could be finer than an authentic Parisian café table and chairs? Maybe we could buy one right from a street on the Left Bank. Or maybe we could find one at Le Café des Etudiants next to the Sorbonne where her father studied medicine and enjoyed café life.

While we were still in Italy, we commissioned our group's American Express agent to purchase a café table, two straw café chairs and a Cinzano ashtray from a café on the Left Bank. It was

August in Paris. The boulevards and cafés were empty. Our agent had no trouble persuading a café owner to part with a used table and chairs. He had them boxed and shipped to the ocean liner that later carried our group across the Atlantic to Montreal.

Back in Stockbridge, I created *Le Café de Maman* behind the barn, decorating the lichen-covered stonewalls with posters of art exhibits and concerts that Ginny and I had collected over the summer. I placed a replica of the *Venus de Milo* at the entrance. French café music filled the air as my parents, my father in a suit and tie and my mother wearing a silk dress, a pill-box hat and a boa, crossed Devon Road from Pilgrims Inn and strolled arm in arm down the grassy slope to the back of the barn. Wearing a beret, one of their friends, Howell Forbes, stood awaiting their arrival, a starched white napkin over his arm. He was holding a silver tray with two tall glasses of Kir Royale, champagne with cassis. The celebration was *un succes fou,* a wild success!

Our daughter Kristin now uses the café table as a telephone table in her home in Garrison, New York. Only one of the straw chairs remains. The Cinzano ashtray has long since disappeared.

During the entire ten-month period before we were married, from August 1959 until June 1960, I spoke with Bud only twice on the telephone, each time for three minutes, a grand total of six minutes of conversation! Overseas phone calls were prohibitively expensive. Holding a three-minute egg timer, I would take the telephone with its long cord into the closet in my dorm room and close the door.

Instead of phone calls, I exchanged letters with Bud. We wrote and wrote, sometimes several letters on the same day, on thin blue airmail stationery. I think a letter took five days to reach Lausanne from Wellesley. It was during the month of November 1959 that we made the decision by mail to marry. Our letters during that month reveal dramatic swings on my part between eagerness to marry and serious doubts. They also reveal the fact that I was very young, age nineteen, and definitely part of a generation of women who assumed that the major role of a wife was to please and care for her husband. I'm reminded of the Turkish Treatment that we sisters had learned to give our father at Pilgrims Inn.

Thus, I was startled recently when I read the following letter written on October 30, 1959. Today, sixty years later, Bud and I are equal partners in marriage. I can't believe that at one time I thought of him as "my lord and master." It was clearly a different world then.

> I feel so sure now, Bud, that I can and will love you forever. I have rid my system of the last dregs of doubt. I know that what we have is too rare and precious for anything but the gentlest and most encouraging care. I want to be with you more than anything in the world and to take care of you . . . This is really all that I want, my darling, and, as you are well aware, I have given it more than my share of thought. And, my lord and master! I have it all planned out! During the day, I will feel like a Queen and will be happy as a lark thinking of you in your business.
>
> Then about four o'clock, I will make you a beautiful dinner and put on a pretty dress, light the candles, put flowers in my hair, and play some Strauss waltzes on the Victrola. Then Bud will come home! And, I will love you forever! With all of my heart! Some days we will read and think and build a fire. Some days we will talk and make plans about

our life and our children's lives. Yes, Bud, suddenly I feel ready for you and love and LIFE.

Bud's response was full of earnest expressions of love and a vision of our life together. My next letter revealed a deep fear that I might not be ready for marriage.

Writing on November 16:

Do you really think that this is right? Sometimes, I get scared and wonder what it will be like in June when we see each other after such a long time? I wonder what marriage means. Does it mean a constant, unerring tenderness and affection for all aspects of marriage and the loved one, or are there times, like the ebb of the tide, when there are doubts and animosity? And, if there are, what does one do? And Bud, let me whisper a question: do you think that we have enough 'common interests' that will endure? Because, I don't want each of us to start going a separate way with only one thing to unite us. Please tell me what you think.

On November 23, Bud responded with what turned out to be the winning letter, the letter that convinced me to marry him:

Now, more than any other time, I'd like to have you here beside me so we could talk together. There are so many things that we should discuss, and letters are so slow, so inadequate, and so easily misunderstood. Darling, I was deeply disturbed and concerned about your last letter, the one in which you 'whispered' your question as to whether I thought we have enough common interests which will endure. It's a good question, a fair question and one that I am glad that you asked. I only wish that you had gone further and, in addition to asking it, had told me a little bit about *your* thoughts on the subject. I sense that you are experiencing doubts or else you probably wouldn't have asked.

Anyway, Za, all I can do in answer to your question is to do my best to tell you how I feel. Let me begin by saying that I think that the concept of 'common interests' is a tricky one. Taken in its narrow, conventional sense, it means that two people are interested in the same intellectual or cultural activities, the same friends and social pastimes, the same sports, the same hobbies, etc. To me these things are important in a good marriage, but not as essential as several other things which I consider much deeper and more basic. First, one of the things that really seems important to me is that a husband and a wife share essentially the same set of beliefs and principles by which they live. Second, I feel that it's important that two people who are joined in marriage should both have good minds, lots of curiosity and energy, and an eagerness to explore new ideas and new activities. This must include a willingness to respect and learn more about each other's interests and ideas. Finally, I think that the most essential common denominator in a marriage and the thing that always keeps a relationship fresh and interesting is LOVE. A mature love, Za, can be a powerful, positive tool. When two people share a mature love for each other, they find that with each other's encouragement, advice, honest criticism and example, they are able to develop their abilities and individual interests to a far greater extent than they thought possible. And, while it might happen that their talents lie in somewhat different directions, they discover that this only tends to make their life together more fascinating . . . for they are always learning new things from one another.

I guess that all I'm trying to say, Za, is that, at this stage of the game, I think that it is far more important that we . . . you and I . . . share the same common set of ideals and fundamentals than that we share a common set of specific interests. The specific interests can only come later, after time and experience and sharing have given us a chance to develop more maturity in our thinking. *Then*, when we speak of interests, we will mean deep, lasting, meaningful interests.

Now then, darling, in answer to your question: I think it may be too early yet to make predictions concerning specific common interests; but when it comes to the really basic ingredients for a marriage that will always be interesting, stimulating, and meaningful, the answer is YES!, we have more than our share. And this is something that I feel strongly and in which I have a very deep faith.

My darling, if I felt that you were completely ready for it, I would give anything in the world to marry you next summer and bring you back to Switzerland. There's only one problem, Za. Need I tell you? Much as it hurts me to say it, I don't think that you are as yet quite ready for marriage. I sense that you feel there are still some things that you want to do or prove to yourself before *settling down* (I hate that term). This is quite natural and as it should be. Nevertheless, my darling, as long as you feel this way, our plans for marriage can and must wait.

I love you, my darling, with all my heart and all my soul . . .

in spite of (or perhaps because of) the fact that you are so very young and still spin in your feelings and attitudes like a weathervane in a capricious wind!

I read the letter and was overcome by Bud's patience, tolerance, and kindness. I replied:

> I read today about the Fillylooloo Bird—the bird that flies backward because it doesn't care where it is going, but it likes to see where it has been. I think that I have been a Fillylooloo Bird about so many things. BUT I AM ONE NO LONGER! My heart is full of an overwhelming love for you. How happy I feel knowing that I have made a decision that will last. I have decided what I am going to do with the needlepoint that I bought yesterday. I am going to use it to cover a footstool, so that I can sit at your feet in the evenings and love you, worship you! Was there ever such a man as you, Bud, for understanding and wisdom. I feel humbled that you have chosen me.

Soon afterwards, Bud wrote to my father asking for my hand in marriage. My father sent him an affirmative response without asking me, as I remember, for my thoughts. It didn't really matter. I had said "Yes!" and was already working on my dowry, a linen bedspread on which, using colored threads, I cross-stitched flowers, birds, and butterflies. There followed an exchange of letters between our parents in which they approved of our plan to marry. Bud's parents wrote to express their support:

> *We are all very happy about the union, for we feel that it will be a sound one based on a foundation of strong love and*

> *mutual respect. We think that we are fortunate in having him marry a girl as fine as Charlotte. We, too, fell in love with her when we met her last June. We think that you will find Bud to be a fine son-in-law. His ideals are high, and he is stable and sincere. I'm sure that he will continue to love Charlotte always and do all in his power to make her happy through the years.*

Sixty-two years have passed since Bud and I met. I was delighted to find and read these letters, glad that I had put them in a shoe box and had not thrown them away. How young I was, how naïve, how trusting, how hopeful, how loving, how excited about life. The letters allowed me the amazing experience of discovering who I was so long ago.

In late November of my junior year, Bud's parents called me from Mansfield, Ohio welcoming me into their family and inviting me to visit them with my parents. They wanted to give an engagement party for me, even though their son was far away in Switzerland.

It was February 1960. I had just turned twenty. Traveling with my parents on my first plane flight, I remember feeling somewhat like a mail-order bride. At the engagement party at the Mansfield Women's Club, with no fiancé at my side and feeling very much alone, I knew that I had to do something to show myself and others that I was engaged to a real person. I had no photographs of Bud. On an impulse, I bought a large cardboard poster to stand beside me in the receiving line. On it, I drew a stick figure to represent Bud. The face was a blank oval, later crayoned over by our children. I propped the poster against a vase of calla lilies on the grand piano and began to greet the guests. The poster was my surrogate husband-to-be.

One afternoon in the late spring of my junior year when I was visiting Pilgrims Inn, my mother said that she wanted to talk with me about marriage. We sat outside on the stone terrace under the lofty ancient birch tree. She handed me a small iridescent seashell. It was exquisite, delicately curled in on itself. "I call this the Yield Shell," she said. "Look at it and remember its message." We studied the shell. "In marriage, you must yield," said my mother.

I quietly absorbed her message, although I remember being bewildered that my mother, my maverick, fun-loving, free-spirited mother whose advice I cherished, was suggesting that this was what marriage would mean for me. In fact, that day the Yield Shell concept seemed like an ominous forecast. Would all exuberance be squeezed out of me when I married? Was I to merge in marriage and then be submerged in the service of my husband, six years older, wiser, and more confident? I had a vague, uneasy, unarticulated feeling that this would be the case.

Today, in our feminist age, it is clear that my mother was a product of a culture where women, except for Queen Victoria, deferred to men. It appeared to be a *quid pro quo:* a wife's submission for the husband's protection and financial support.

In my mother's talk that day, nothing was said about the over-arching and balancing privilege found in a good marriage: the joy of being able to love and care for someone and the joy and comfort of feeling loved and cared for in return. Or that vitality, excitement, spontaneity, even freedom, could be found, maybe even enhanced, within a marriage.

Although I had these feelings and although I removed the word "Obey" from the Episcopal Church's marriage vows for the bride, I remained true to the prevailing culture and to the message of the Yield Shell. My wedding gift to Bud was a small brass pot from Nepal that looked like Aladdin's lamp. I had it inscribed with "*Thy Whim is My Command.*" Bud was to rub it three times and I would appear to answer his wishes. Later, after we had married and were living in an apartment in Lausanne, Switzerland, I put his slippers and pipe and this magic lamp near a comfortable chair to greet him upon his return from work.

Charlotte Bronte, author of *Jane Eyre*, published in 1847, once wrote to a friend: "*It is a solemn and strange and perilous thing for a woman to become a wife.*" Although I was passionately in love with Bud and imagined sharing a long life with him, I had similar thoughts as I was seriously contemplating marriage. I was scared of the unfamiliar territory that I might be entering. "*There Be Dragons*" was written on the uncharted territories of early maps. As reflected in the following letter written in the spring of 1960, marriage was definitely uncharted territory for me and, therefore, worthy of some deep thought:

> Do you know something, Bud? I listened tonight to an old speech of Thomas Jefferson's, written at the birth of America. Highly moral and idealistic in tone—the new child beginning life with the world, everything open in front of her. That is how I consider our life. Now, at the start, the basic choices and the ideals which we establish will be of utmost significance. We both have an immense amount to give and a great deal of idealism. Let us never allow ourselves to slide into *mediocrity*, but let us make something of real consequence out of our lives—for others.

> In the first few years of our married life, we will be establishing a pattern, laying the foundation for the rest of it. It will be a challenge, Bud, I know. Let's not establish security and conformity and restraint as our talismans, even though I fear that the demands of our society can gradually bend, then bind the individual. Maybe you fear this, too, as you suggested when you said you disliked the term *settling down*.

Before the wedding, as was traditional, I ordered ivory-colored calling cards embossed with *Mrs. Ralph Z. Sorenson*. Even then, this felt odd. On the one hand, as a young woman of the time, I felt proud to have been "chosen." On the other hand, at a deeper level, I missed my own familiar name. I seldom used those calling cards.

Many years later, in my seventies, I designed my own personal calling card. On the sparkling talcum-powder sand in the Yucatan, Mexico, I noticed and photographed a coral-colored blossom. Beside it, on my new card, I printed *Charlotte Ripley Sorenson*, my first name, my maiden name and my married name. It's hard to explain, but with that card, I felt at long last that I had fully embraced my identity.

Recently, I came across a small plain white card that we students may have exchanged at Wellesley. It was printed with my full maiden name, *Charlotte Bacon Ripley*. Perhaps the three cards show a symbolic progression into selfhood. I am glad that today's young women can choose to keep their own names when they marry or they can choose the pre-fix, *Ms.* instead of *Mrs.*

With both Bud's and my parents solidly behind our union, a wedding date was chosen, June 25, 1960. Preparations began immediately. Whom should we invite to the wedding? Whom should we invite to the parties? What about the wedding dress? Should I wear the one that my paternal grandmother and my mother had worn? Who could make it fit? What about flowers? Music? Bridesmaids?

I felt as though I were in a coach that was rolling and had no brakes. In the words of the song of the day: "*Love and marriage, love and marriage, go together like a horse and carriage. This I'm telling you, brother, you can't have one without the other.*" There was no turning back.

I had concerns during these wedding preparations, especially as I could not communicate easily with Bud. There were times when I felt overwhelmed with doubts and fears. Even so, I yearned to be with him again. I had faith in the love Bud expressed in his letters and his sincere commitment to our life together. I had faith in Bud. And I loved him.

With great excitement, then, on June 15, 1960, just ten days before our wedding, I welcomed Bud at La Guardia Airport in New York City. We boarded a public bus for Stockbridge where we spent just two days together before Bud flew to Ohio to spend a week with his family. I was thrilled and comforted to see him after so much time apart, but I was still anxious about the step that I was about to take. Decisions had been made for me all of my life. I was aware that this was the first major decision and choice I had ever been asked to make. And, in my mind, it would be for life.

My emotions were in turmoil on the day before the wedding, soaring at the thought of a committed life with Bud and plunging into confusion and dread at the step that I was about to take. I told Bud that we needed to talk. We walked to a meadow on Rattlesnake Mountain.

Brimming with confidence, positive energy, and a sense of purpose, Bud was different from any of the young men I had met. I admired and was drawn to his special qualities, so different from mine. Maybe, as I had written, we didn't have enough interests in common. Perhaps, because of our differences, we weren't suited to each other. I voiced my concerns once again and even suggested that maybe we should call off the wedding. Maybe we should spend more time together, getting to know one another before we married. In addition, I told him that several respected friends of my parents had written to me suggesting that it would be a mistake for me to marry before finishing college. Somehow, in his reassuring way, Bud convinced me that we were meant for each other and that all would be well. The coach continued to roll toward its destination, gathering speed.

The church bells pealed on June 25, 1960. My wedding bouquet was a bouffant mix of daisies, white roses, mountain laurel, and edelweiss. The bridesmaids carried long stems of blue delphinium. My wedding dress, worn by both my Ripley grandmother and my mother had been hemmed and tucked. My father walked me down the aisle at Saint Paul's Episcopal Church. My sisters, Ginny and Anne, were bridesmaids along with Bud's sister, Nancy. My brothers, George and Franklin, ages twelve and eight, were in the wedding party.

After the service, my mother sent an emergency vehicle to pick up the wedding cake that she had forgotten at the bakery. It arrived just in time for the informal reception on the lawn behind Pilgrims Inn. Bud and I stood under the rose arbor to greet our guests. We cut the wedding cake with the Ripley family's engraved Civil War sword.

Beyond these details, and the fact that the sun was shining and that there were many gracious, smiling people in attendance, I remember almost nothing of our wedding day. Clemens Kalischer, a professional photographer, a resident of Stockbridge, and a family friend, took beautiful photographs which capture that remarkable day.

After I had thrown my bouquet from the front balcony, Bud and I left Pilgrims Inn in a blue Volkswagen Bug with "Just Married" painted on the side and tin cans clanging noisily behind. We spent our first night as a married couple at the Lord Jeffrey Amherst Inn in Amherst, Massachusetts. Amherst College was Bud's *alma mater.* I was so unprepared for the sexual aspect of marriage that I pulled a Bible from the drawer in the table by the bed and suggested that maybe we could just pray.

The following week, we luxuriated in a small cabin near South Beach in Chilmark on Martha's Vineyard. We then flew to Spain, to the island of Majorca where we stayed in the Hotel Bendinat on the Mediterranean coast. We planned to go from there to Switzerland where we would live for at least a year. It was an incredible honeymoon. Like mist vanishing under a warm morning sun, my doubts and fears about Bud and marriage miraculously evaporated.

Years later, while traveling in South Korea, we visited a restoration of a South Korean village where I watched a presentation of a traditional Korean wedding. The Korean bride, heavily veiled, was placed on a cushion in a curtained ceremonial box lashed to two long wooden poles. Four strong men hoisted the box onto their shoulders and carried the bride to her fate. I felt a sudden flash of empathy. I remembered how I had felt on the morning of my wedding day as people hovered around, dressing me, fixing my hair, fastening my necklace, "preparing me." My culture, my group, my family, and finally, even I myself—unlike the Korean bride—had made the decision that would create my destiny.

My decision to marry Bud has led to an extraordinarily beautiful life that has lasted for six decades. The curtains that I pulled back on my symbolic box on our wedding day revealed a sparkling future filled with adventure and learning, beauty, and love. It has been a joyful journey.

Portrait of my maternal grandfather,
Dr. John Bergeson (1864–1927)
Painted in Paris in 1895 by Jules Fachnlein
when my grandfather was studying medicine
at the Sorbonne.

My maternal grandmother,
Charlotte Lucy True Bergeson (1877–1957)
A teacher and a talented artist, she lived
in Newton Center, Massachusetts with her
husband and three children.

My paternal grandparents, Philip Franklin Ripley (1876–1955)
and Mabel Genevra Bacon Ripley (1874–1949)
He was a graduate of Yale, Class of 1897, and a chemist. She was a graduate of Smith College, Class of 1896, a teacher and a classics scholar. They lived in Andover, Massachusetts.

Part Two

Photo Album

My father, George Ripley (1911–1987)
Banker, explorer, sportsman, a true
Yankee gentleman. Settled in Stockbridge,
Massachusetts.

My mother, Ruth Bergeson Ripley (1912–2004)
Wellesley College, Class of 1934. With her
warmth and wit, she was the inspiration
behind Pilgrims Inn.

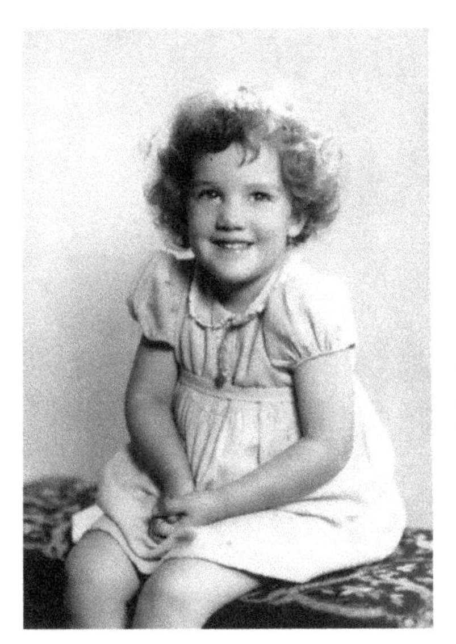

Three years old

My mother and father reading to my sister,
Virginia True Ripley, and to me. Our
education began at an early age.

The Ripley and Bergeson Families
Front row, left to right: my paternal grandmother, Mabel Genevra Bacon, Charlotte, my sister Anne on my mother's lap, my sister Ginny, my maternal grandmother, Charlotte Lucy True Bergeson. Back row: My father, George Ripley, his sister, Helen (Aunt H) in her Navy uniform, his sister Susan, and my paternal grandfather, Philip Franklin Ripley.

The three Ripley sisters, fascinated by the world: Anne with her finger on the globe, Ginny, standing and Charlotte, kneeling and locating a special spot, maybe Switzerland or the Philippines.

Artist's rendering of Pilgrims Inn, Stockbridge, Massachusetts

Photo of our granddaughter, Tessa True Peterson, dressed for her great-grandmother's memorial service, standing in front of the historic Pilgrims Inn sign.

All doubts vanquished! Shortly before our wedding on June 25, 1960.
Photo by Clemens Kalischer

Ready for Life! After the wedding ceremony and the ringing of the church bells, Bud and I leave St. Paul's Church, Stockbridge, to begin our life together. My sister Anne is in the background.
Photo by Clemens Kalischer

View over vineyards, Lake Geneva and the French Alps from our balcony at Modern City A, Lausanne, Switzerland.

"The hills are alive . . ." Filled with joy in an alpine meadow.

Happy days! Skiing above the clouds in Switzerland.

Hiking in the Alps with Kristin Elizabeth, born in Lausanne on April 14, 1962.

Manila, Philippines. 1966.
Our family in a nipa hut, a traditional Philippine stilt house.

Our wonderful helper, Gloria, pulling Kristin and Trina around San Lorenzo Village in Manila on a papier-mâché horse.

Charlotte learning to perform the Philippine national folk dance, Tininkling or the Bamboo Dance. With Professor J.B. Kassarjian, a member of the Harvard Advisory Group.

Charlotte arriving at one of the many fancy parties in Manila.

July 1967. Sorenson and Ripley families at Pilgrims Inn during our six-week home leave from the Philippines. Front row: Kristin, my brother, George, my mother, my father, his sister Helen (Aunt H), my sister Ginny holding her daughter Lucy Hathaway. Back row: my brother Franklin, a friend, my sister Anne. I am holding Eric and Bud is holding Trina.

The Babson College President's Residence in Wellesley, Massachusetts where our family lived for seven years (1974–1981) and where we entertained about 2,000 guests a year.

Firing the gun to start the women's cross-country race. 1978 Babson International Student Olympics.

"In Stillness There is a Song"
Seated in the Meditation Retreat on the shore of Lake Waban
that Bud and I donated to Wellesley College in 2006.

Celebrating in nineteenth century style with my Wellesley College classmates. We dressed in white and carried parasols at Edith Wharton's historic home in Lenox, Massachusetts.

The Meadow. Kristin, Eric and Trina and a red parasol in our flower-filled meadow overlooking the Berkshire Hills in Stockbridge, Massachusetts.

Boulder, Colorado. Family at Red Rocks in 1995, three years after we had moved to Boulder. Jess Peterson, Trina's husband, is holding our first grandchild, Soren Shipp Peterson.

View from the Petersons' home on Glacier Lake. Nederland, Colorado. In the distance is the South Arapaho Peak on the Continental Divide.

Our Monet-inspired bridge over the historic Farmers Ditch in Boulder.

On the steps of the magic shack during my quest for enlightenment in Tulum, Yucatan, Mexico.

We have been blessed. Standing under a rainbow near Victoria Falls, Zimbabwe, Africa.

Part Three

1960–2019

Chapter Five

Life in Europe

and Home
(1960–1964)

For the first three years of our marriage, because of Bud's work at IMEDE and then at Nestle's headquarters in Vevey, we lived in Lausanne, Switzerland. What follows are snapshots of our life and travels in Europe during that time.

A few months after her marriage, Charlotte Bronte wrote again to a friend: "*I have a good, kind and attached husband, and every day makes my attachment to him stronger.*" I concurred. Bud and I were blissfully happy. We were rhapsodic about our new life together. I wrote long letters to my family describing our apartments, our friends, and our explorations in the Swiss and, eventually, the European countryside.

We lived for the first few months with a vineyard-keeper, a *vigneron*, Monsieur Damazat, in La Conversion above the lakeside town of Pully. From our balcony, we looked out over Lake Geneva and beyond to the Dents du Midi, mountains in France that towered 10,000 feet above the lake. Gazing to the left, we looked down the Valais, the valley carved by the Rhone River. To the right, on a crystal-clear day, we could see the Jet d'Eau, the tall water plume rising from the lake in Geneva.

Another tenant in our vineyard apartment was Hilmar Bussacker, a refugee from East Berlin who had fled his home just before the construction of the Berlin Wall in August 1961. Hilmar knew that if he tried to return to visit his family, he would risk being captured by the Communist government and either jailed or put to death. In spite of the peril, he disguised himself at one point with a long black beard and glasses and managed to cross the border for a brief visit. He returned with tales of the bleak, impoverished life behind the Iron Curtain.

At IMEDE, the 1960–1961 executive management program included participants from Europe and around the world, among them an Egyptian, a Scandinavian, a Lebanese, a South African, a Brazilian, and a Swiss who had been working in the Congo. A Vietnamese poet wandered around at receptions with a packet of blank cards on which he wrote and dedicated a poem to each female guest. I was impressed that he had just finished translating *Dr. Zhivago* from Russian into Vietnamese. During the final reception, he gave a fake pearl to each guest. We then strung them on a single string symbolizing our eternal connection. One of our favorite friends was Angelo Tagliavia, a dark, volatile Sicilian, who was married to Sheila, a slender, cerebral Canadian with blonde hair and a cool intellect.

While we lived in Lausanne, we were always aware, of course, of what was happening in the United States: the November 1960 election of President John F. Kennedy, the catastrophic defeat of the CIA-trained Americans in their conflict with Fidel Castro in the Bay of Pigs in April 1961, and the Cuban Missile Crisis in October 1962. Even though the Swiss government responded to each of the Cuban incidents by limiting the sale of sugar and staples in the markets, for us America's problems with Cuba seemed distant. To protect its population from possible wartime deprivation, however, we learned that the Swiss government mandates even today that each household and apartment building include a fall-out shelter stocked with water and provisions from a list provided by the government. To ensure freshness, the provisions are to be replaced every few months.

Perhaps because of our lack of exposure to a land war in our own country, World War II became intensely real to us. The war had ended only fifteen years earlier and its horrors were still very much on people's minds. Bombings had devastated cities. Tank and gun fighting had bloodied European lands and traumatized its people. We began to hear chilling stories about the rise of Adolf Hitler, his brutal, grotesque treatment of Jews and other minorities and the hellish conditions in the concentration camps. Many of the Europeans whom we met seemed war-weary and cynical, in contrast to most Americans, myself included, who were uninformed politically and astonishingly naïve, trusting, and idealistic.

Switzerland had not directly participated in World War II. Its status of permanent neutrality had been established in 1815 by the Treaty of Paris. Even so we found reminders of the war in strange places. Once when we were driving through a narrow pass in the Valais, I was certain that the side of the mountain was moving. We stopped the car and clambered up the steep slope. Indeed, a heavy canvas cover, camouflaged with painted vegetation, had torn loose from the rock wall. Behind the flapping curtain was a deep cavern that had served as a military cannon emplacement. Switzerland, we learned, has miles and miles of underground caverns and tunnels holding hospitals, arsenals, and living spaces. Sometimes on a drive you might see a small window pierced high into a rock face, a clue to living spaces deep inside the mountain.

On another occasion on the road to Geneva, we passed a large farmhouse. I thought something looked strange. We stopped the car to investigate. Every window was covered with a lace curtain, but it turned out that the lace curtains were not real. The lacey-design was painted on the glass. And why were there so many fire escapes from the second floor? We learned that this farmhouse had housed Swiss militia during the war. The soldiers needed privacy and quick exits. It was still being used by soldiers doing their military service, required of all able-bodied male citizens over the age of sixteen. Today, Swiss women can also serve in the military as volunteers.

After a few months in the vineyard, we moved to 9 Avenue Floreal in Ouchy near the shore of Lake Geneva and close to IMEDE. The concierge, a small man with narrow glittery eyes, closely watched the comings and the goings in the building. He kept a string of garlic cloves hanging in the elevator and chewed a clove several times a day.

Peter Brooke, an Englishman and colleague of Bud's, brought his parents to stay with us for several days in our tiny apartment. His gentle, modest parents were the Right Honorable Henry Brooke, British Home Secretary and Dame Barbara Brooke, Vice-Chairman of the British Conservative Party. Their friend, Lancelot Fleming, the Bishop of Norwich, stayed with us as well. We took them on picnics and introduced them to Lausanne.

After a year or so, Bud accepted a job at the Nestle Company as assistant to the world-wide head of marketing. We moved again to an apartment building called Modern City A, in Pully-La-Rosiaz, a small town above Lausanne. It was an odd name for a building that had a panoramic view of Lake Geneva, a tennis court, and an excellent location, just a short walk from a boulangerie, a charcuterie, a fromagerie, and small shops selling fresh vegetables, flowers and wine. Food shopping was an everyday affair. *"Bonjour, Madame."* The shopkeepers would welcome you in provincial, sing-song French.

In the Swiss fashion, the sidewalks in front of the shops were swept and washed clean every day and the shop windows polished. I rarely spotted a weed during our stay in Lausanne. Flowers in window boxes and in the formal garden beds in Ouchy showed no sign of wilt or decay. Diseased leaves must have been meticulously removed at night. In the streets, Swiss policemen in impeccable uniforms directed traffic with stiff, almost mechanical gestures.

We made a number of Swiss friends, but I observed that the Swiss were frugal and exacting in their interpersonal exchanges. If you borrowed an egg from a neighbor, I learned that you had to note whether it was brown or white and whether it was small, medium or large. You were expected to return an identical egg. When we left Modern City A in 1963, our landlord who had come to inspect the apartment asked us to estimate how much light was left in the light bulbs. When we confessed that we were unsure, he insisted that we replace all of the light bulbs with new ones. I had worked hard to leave the apartment in perfect condition. I burst into tears, unable to believe his pettiness.

I was twenty when we arrived in Switzerland. Bud was often away, visiting European companies and writing case studies for IMEDE. I was lonely that first year when he was traveling. Some days I cried, homesick for my family and my college friends. I began to study the violin, but that only increased my feelings of isolation. Life became more interesting when I enrolled in the *Ecole de Francais Moderne* at the University of Lausanne. I practiced my French in the markets and shops. Even without a work visa, I eventually found a job teaching English at the *Ecole Benedict* to a class of rambunctious boys of my age who had failed the Swiss National Exam. One day, they lit a smoke bomb in the back of the classroom causing me to faint dead away behind my desk.

For fun, Bud and I took drawing lessons from David Burnand, a *vigneron* and artist. Once a week, we climbed rickety wooden steps to his *atelier* filled with dust and cobwebs and unidentifiable objects. The ancient stove leaked ashes, a green bottle decorated to look like a fish hung from the ceiling, old squashed hats dangled from nails, the spring-less couch for the model was stacked with pillows and tattered gray blankets. We would spend two hours with students and aspiring artists from every walk of life making pencil and charcoal sketches of a nude model. A be-speckled and be-caped elderly artist named M. Voegli, a female student wearing black pants and a green sweater, and others floated around smoking pipes and sharpening their pencils. The cost of the session was the Swiss franc equivalent of twenty-five cents, enough to pay the model and keep the iron stove filled with wrinkled old vines from David's vineyard.

Or we would attend the tiny theater at the foot of the wooden stairs leading up to the Cathedral of Lausanne. We always sat in the front row where we could see the big looping stitches in the homemade costumes and hear the back-stagers prompting the actors and whispering about the faulty lighting and the raggedy curtain. I loved it. In the tiny chapel in the lakeside town of San Sulpice, we watched with consternation one Christmas Eve as the priest in a flowing white cassock climbed a tall, wobbly, homemade wooden ladder and reached out with a long taper to light the candles on the tree. The four fresco'd apostles in the apse seemed frozen in apprehension, too.

In the evenings, we would sometimes see the satellite Sputnik pass overhead. A Russian satellite, in orbit since 1957, it was the first satellite to orbit the earth. The Space Race between the United States and Russia was underway. We were full of wonder at this technological penetration of the skies.

On weekends, we explored the countryside of Switzerland, a small federation of twenty-six cantons. Although English is widely spoken, there are four official languages: German, French, Italian and Romansch. We once visited the canton of Appenzell where in a referendum in 1959, just a year before we arrived, sixty-seven percent of the country's male voters had denied Swiss women the right to vote in federal elections. We watched the election in the town square. Men had to carry either a sword or a dagger. They voted by raising an arm. It was not until February 1971, in fact, that Swiss women were given the right to vote.

"It's a castle! I know it's a castle! Over there!" I exclaimed. We stopped the car on a side road in the rolling hills of the Jura and started hiking toward the distant turrets. As we approached the town with its medieval castle, the smell of baking bread filled the air. We easily found the bakery and the fromagerie, stuffed our hot loaves of bread with cheese and splurged on this molten delicacy as we hiked back to our car. Switzerland is full of storybook towns with narrow, cobblestoned streets, and forts and castles with moats and crenellated walls. I delighted in exploring them with Bud.

We feasted on cheese fondue in the fortified medieval town of Gruyere. We explored the Chateau de Chillon on Lake Geneva where, according to Lord Byron, prisoners had been chained to the dungeon walls. I was charmed by the Chateau d'Oron with its intimate library and leather folios containing exquisite botanical drawings. We explored Roman ruins and Romanesque churches.

In the spring, we picnicked in ravishing alpine meadows, wildly fragrant with snowy white narcissi. We went on long hikes, once from Gstaad to Meiringen. We climbed the Eggishorn and almost died coming down the un-marked, scree-filled back side. During the winter months, we skied in Verbier, Villars, and Zermatt on long wooden skis without safety bindings, not mandatory in those days. Our woolen gloves and leather boots quickly became soggy and cold. Even so, it was exhilarating to be skiing in the dazzling frosty air above the clouds.

One rainy afternoon, we crossed Lake Geneva on a passenger ferry from Lausanne to Evian-les-Bains, a French watering hole. In the spacious central room of the spa, we observed dozens of Europeans soberly and conscientiously taking the water cure to cleanse their livers of foie gras, fine wines, and pastries. Each guest was assigned a chair with an armrest large enough to hold a glass. It was a sodden, dismal scene. Rain streaked the windows. Guests sat in silence staring at the falling rain, sipping glass after glass of Evian water. In the center of the room was a fountain with many spouts where one could get a refill. In a corner of the room, an amateur string quartet sawed away off-key, their instruments out of tune in the damp air.

We traveled outside the country as well, changing our Swiss francs, at the time four francs to the dollar, into the local currency as we went. Usually there were barriers and border controls. We always carried our passports. The Schengen Agreement (signed in 1985) would later create an area of twenty-six European countries where people could travel freely without passports or border controls. It was not in effect, however, until 1995, thirty-two years after we had left Europe.

In 1961, we spent our second European Christmas in Norway with my sister, Ginny. I remember the seven kinds of Christmas cookies served on every occasion. I remember singing and dancing around a candlelit tree and the spectacular *kransekake* made of crushed almonds that Ginny had created to celebrate my twenty-first birthday. I remember the hatred that the Norwegians expressed for Germany and for the Germans who had occupied their country during the war. I remember the moist eye of the fresh codfish peering through the fishmonger's wrapping paper before it was rendered into a Christmas pudding.

I remember being five months pregnant that Christmas with our first child, Kristin, and being told that in order to protect my baby I had to keep my knees warm, above all! I remember speeding through the snowy countryside on New Year's Day in a train car communicating with smiles and hand gestures with a friendly group of deaf-mutes. We disembarked in Tvedestrand, a beautiful small town on the Oslo fjord, and walked the snowy streets trying to find Bud's grandfather's home. We spent the night under comforters in a frigid hotel room overlooking the frozen harbor. The hotel had been closed for the season, but the manager had taken pity on us when he had seen us walking with our suitcases at dusk on the frozen streets. He opened a guest room for us and brought us a tray of Christmas cookies. I remember that the knee warmers, given to me in Oslo, kept slipping down to my ankles. The next morning, holding onto an old black and white photograph of the house and trying to match landmarks with the house, we eventually found Bud's grandfather's house, #28 Osterkliev. It was a small, white clapboard house above the harbor in the charming old part of town.

Another trip took us across the English Channel to visit the Brookes who had invited us to stay with them in Hampstead in London. Dame Barbara brought tea to us in our room first thing each morning before retiring to her room with the morning papers. The Right Honorable Henry, Bud, and I had quiet breakfasts together of ham, eggs, bacon, tomatoes, and dry cold toast served in a silver toast holder. To complete the meal, of course, there was orange marmalade and more tea. I watched as the Home Secretary browsed through the pile of newspapers on the table. The headlines excoriated him and his policies. He showed no emotion as he read, seemingly unaffected by the intense public criticism.

Dame Barbara took me with her one day to the House of Commons where our dear host was jeered and sneered at for his housing policies. He had warned us to expect this derision as part of normal parliamentary procedure. Prime Minister MacMillan spoke of the possible establishment of a Polaris missile base off the coast of Scotland and of his talks with Eisenhower on this subject. We watched from the balcony as Sir Winston Churchill entered the chamber to thunderous applause and the stamping of feet. He was short and stocky and carried a cane. He smiled broadly and raised his arms in a victory salute. It was one of his last appearances in the House of Commons.

Nearby, in the House of Lords, we listened to a discussion of the advantages of changing pounds and shillings, the English currency, to the metric system. Many of the aristocratic Lords were nodding or were actually asleep. The Lords were mostly silver-haired and wearing carnations in their buttonholes while the active, pragmatic members of the House of Commons wore heather colored, Shetland sweaters.

Dame Barbara and I became friends. We exchanged letters over the years. She once wrote me a note that ended: "Faithfulness in small things is a great thing." I tried to keep that in mind during the years that I was raising children and keeping house.

During the late summer of 1959, when my sister Ginny and I were traveling on our own in Europe, we had a brief visit with the Guschlbauer family in Vienna, Austria. Just after World War II, my Ripley grandparents had sent CARE packages to the Guschlbauer family, an intellectual family of scientists, musicians, and engineers. CARE was an American relief program that sent parcels of food to Europeans who were at risk of starving.

I had described this special family in a letter to Bud dated November 20, 1959, during the month when we were deciding whether or not to marry.

> Do you remember that Ginny and I visited the Guschlbauer family last summer? Frau with her knitting, Herr und Hans laughing and telling jokes, musical Dorli intent on following the bass line in a musical piece. The family has really suffered from the war with its dangers and poverty . . . and yet they give, give, give. They don't seem to need much to be happy. It's the love and humility that count. I'm convinced that they have found the secret of life. They live in their plain apartment on the fourth floor of an old building, three children and the parents. Yet the rooms don't seem crowded. They never complain. The rooms are filled with music and intelligent conversation and love. I want you to meet them. They are such a rare family. Perhaps we could model our family after theirs.

The Guschlbauers learned that Bud and I were living in Lausanne and invited us to visit them in their apartment in Vienna. Their family of five or six lived in a tiny walk-up apartment that was spare and simply furnished. The parents, in an extremely generous gesture, insisted that Bud and I sleep in their bed.

The devastation of war was alarmingly visible in Vienna which had been heavily bombed. Young, sensitive Teodore "Dorli" Guschlbauer, a cellist, took us on a tour of the city, guiding us past bombed-out buildings. Even fifteen years after the Armistice, the city seemed dead. Herr und Frau Guschlbauer told us stories of surviving on the few potatoes and turnips that they would collect on walks outside the city. As a wedding gift, the family presented us with a green leather guestbook. On the first page Dorli inscribed music from Mozart's *The Magic Flute* and the words: "*In diesen heiligen hallen . . .*" ("In these holy halls, man knows no revenge; and, if a man has fallen, Love leads him to his duty.")

Many years later, Dorli stayed with us in Wellesley when he came to Boston with a Youth Orchestra. Years passed. One afternoon when we were living in Cambridge, I was listening to a classical music station on the radio. After a Brahms concerto, I heard, "Conducted by Teodore Guschlbauer, Chef d'Orchestra of the Strasburg Philharmonic Orchestra." Bravo, Dorli!

In Grenada, Spain, in the exquisite gardens of the Alhambra, we acted out the parts of Boabdil, the twelfth century Sultan of Grenada, and Zaida, his Muslim mistress. For reference, we had with us a copy of Washington Irving's *Tales of the Alhambra*. In Madrid, we learned how the Spanish general and dictator Francisco Franco had been supported by German Nazis and Italian Fascists during the Spanish Civil War (1936–1939.) Franco ruled for thirty-six years until he died in 1975. Politics was clearly a subject of heated debate in Europe where Nazis, Fascists and Communists had all recently threatened democratic institutions.

In his 1961 inaugural address, President John F. Kennedy implored American citizens: "Ask not what your country can do for you; ask what you can do for your country." Perhaps Winston Churchill could have inspired his people with this idealistic plea, but at the time I couldn't think of those words being spoken by any other European leader, all of whom appeared to have been hardened and jaded by the two world wars recently fought on their soil.

In Europe, in fact, we seemed to be witnesses to war wherever we went, even from our balcony in Modern City A. Charles de Gaulle, the President of France, had declared in 1954 that the Algerians in North Africa had a right to be independent like their neighbors in Morocco and Tunisia. Of course, the French living in Algeria (the *Pieds-Noirs*) profited from the fact that Algeria was a French colony and pressed their cause with terrorism and violence. The OAS (*Organization de l'Armee Secrete*), a French right-wing group, also fought for almost eight years guerrilla-style against Algerian independence.

I have a distinct memory of the signing of the Evian Accords on March 18, 1962, as it was the month before our daughter Kristin was born. "*Algerie pour les Algeriens*" had been the cry. Now, finally, the Algerians had their independence. The French-Algerian War had ended. The Pieds-Noirs fled from Algeria back to France. After a week or so of random celebratory gunfire, the Evian Accords were signed in Evian, France. We stood on our balcony in Modern City A and watched and listened to the enormous display of fireworks and military salutes exploding on the far side of Lake Geneva.

Of course, nothing compared to the fireworks and joyous celebrations that took place on April 14, 1962 when Kristin Elizabeth Sorenson was born! Bud and I had prepared for the birth by practicing the Lamaze method of natural childbirth, common in Europe but not yet in the United States. Bud was present at the birth. To keep him occupied and to steady his nerves, the obstetrician offered him a glass of cognac and had him administer oxygen. In La Clinique des Charmettes in Lausanne, a new mother was kept in bed for ten days.

On the day of Kristin's birth, it seemed that all of Nature stood at attention. Birds chorused, flowers bloomed in unusual profusion, the sun smiled. Telegrams flew back and forth across the Atlantic. Letters to our families describe the elation we felt gazing at our beautiful, healthy Kristin in her lacey bassinette. Friends came to gaze and congratulate, bringing wine and smoking cigarettes. Gauloises. Nobody in those days considered the health dangers of second-hand smoke.

Back in our apartment, Hanne Moser, a trained nurse and a family friend who had agreed to be Kristin's godmother, wrapped Kristin carefully in swaddling clothes, a Swiss custom, and showed us how to take care of her. We needed someone to help with the cloth diapers that had to be soaked and washed in the basement, then carried up to the roof to dry in the sun. Christa Schradi came to help.

Lovely Christa, who was in her mid-twenties, was uncomfortable around men. She was unable to face or to walk past them. She told me that she had been raped by a French priest while he was visiting in Germany. She had become pregnant and was in hiding in Switzerland, afraid to face her family. She planned to give birth over the border in France, then put the baby up for adoption. In my protected life, I had never heard a story such as hers. To have been raped was horrific, but to have been raped by a priest, a self-described man of God, was unbelievable. It was my introduction to the hypocrisy of the Catholic Church and its celibate priests. Later, Christa sent us a photo of the baby. "She has red hair," she wrote, "just like the father."

Sometime during that year, I wrote to Dean Theresa Frisch at Wellesley College, requesting that I be allowed to return in September 1963 to complete my senior year. Dean Frisch, a distinguished Austrian art historian, wrote back saying that I could enroll but that I would have to agree not to linger on the campus or mingle with students after my classes. The problem was, I inferred, that I was married and had a child. I had had SEX! It was ten years before Wellesley created the Continuing Education Program for women who wanted a Wellesley education later in their lives.

The Dean's response reminded me of the situation that my grandmother, Mabel Genevra Bacon Ripley, faced when she became pregnant and was forced to give up teaching at Abbot Academy. Feeling that a pregnant instructor would be a bad influence on young female students, the school administrators asked her to resign.

Years later in Boulder, Colorado, I stopped on our street to talk to a neighbor. We found that we had both graduated from Wellesley in 1964. I told her that while I should have graduated in 1961, I had lived in Switzerland for three years and had a child when I returned to Wellesley for my senior year. She looked at me. "Oh, you're the one," she said. "We were told about you during student orientation in the fall." According to my neighbor, implicit in these remarks was a strong suggestion that my fellow students not socialize with me.

Learning that I could return to Wellesley to complete my senior year and that Bud had been accepted in the doctoral program at HBS, we knew that it was time to leave. We packed our belongings in our blue Volkswagen Bug, waved good-by to our neighbors in Modern City A, and drove through France with our precious Kristin and my mother who had been visiting us.

Driving across the border from Switzerland into France was always to me a study in national character. Switzerland is fantastically well-organized, manicured, every inch of land intentionally developed for a useful purpose. Just inside the French border, you immediately notice the difference. The landscape is unkempt, more exuberant, and spontaneous. There are tumble-down forests where dead branches have not been hauled away and towns with moss growing lustily between the cobblestones.

In Le Havre, we boarded the S.S. *France* for the Atlantic crossing, an elegant improvement over the S.S. *Arkadia.* Traveling across the Atlantic by air was still unusual in those days.

Back in Wellesley, we lived at 84 Crest Road on the second floor of a house belonging to Mrs. Barnicle, an elderly, alcoholic widow. While our apartment was close to the campus, our living situation was difficult. Mrs. Barnicle would creep up the open stairwell to spy on us. In distress, I told a friend, "She is omniscient. She reads our mail. She knows everything. We try to toss off her spying with laughter, but she is beginning to drive us crazy." We lived that year on $300 a month. To cover the cost of the Wellesley tuition, I had been given a federal student loan for $1,000. I had ten years to pay it off with a low interest rate. If I went into teaching, the loan would be forgiven. Bud and I proudly paid it off over time in small increments.

During the weekdays on my way to class, I would put Kristin on the back of my bicycle and drop her off to spend the day with Grammy Arsenault, a kind, gray-haired woman with one leg who sat in the middle of her disorganized house and sang and read to her gleeful, unrestrained charges. She told me that she thought that Kristin had the energy to be "the first woman president." That was the first time in my life that I had heard this possibility expressed, that a woman might even be considered for the highest office in the land. Today in 2019, the chance of a woman becoming president is more than just a dream, but it is still elusive.

In the afternoons, even in the snowy winter dusk, to escape Mrs. Barnicle's prying eyes, I would put Kristin in the stroller and push her to the street corner near Route 9 where we would meet Bud coming home from HBS. I kept faith with Dean Frisch's request and did not remain on the Wellesley campus after classes.

It was November 22, 1963. In our tiny apartment, I was listening to the radio after lunch when the announcer broke in. "President Kennedy has just been shot and killed in Dallas, Texas." It was 12:30 pm in Dallas. I dashed down the stairs, jumped on my bike and raced to my class in Political Science. I was late. "President Kennedy has just been killed," I announced breathlessly when I walked in. No one had yet heard the news. The students were stunned, but not our professor: "Those things happen," he said in a world-weary voice. "The class will go on." But not for me. "How can you say that?" I confronted him and walked out of the door, followed by a number of my classmates. We needed time to process the news and to grieve. There wasn't a car or a person on the streets of the town of Wellesley that night when I went to the laundromat to do my wash.

The school year finally ended. On June 8, 1964, Commencement Day, my sister Ginny climbed the bell tower on the Wellesley campus and played the carillon, filling the air with glorious sound. Visibly pregnant with our second daughter, Katrina, I walked onto the stage to receive my diploma while Kristin shouted from the audience, "That's my mommy." A bit uncomfortable, I imagine, for Dean Frisch, who doubtless was in attendance.

In fact, it was a delightful surprise for me a few months later when I received a hand-written letter from Miss Teresa G. Frisch. The letter was dated October 3, 1964:

> *Dearest Charlotte,*
>
> *Felicitations to you and to your dear husband. I was delighted to hear that Katrina Ann has safely arrived. You did so beautifully with your first little daughter that it deserved a repeat performance! I hope that you are back home by now and established in your Cambridge house. I shall love to come and see you and the children sometime this fall....*
>
> *Much love to you—take care of yourself. With my good wishes.*
>
> *Yours, Teresa Frisch*

We spent that hot, humid summer on the shore of Wellesley's Lake Waban, house-sitting for a Wellesley history professor. My major task was trying to stay cool while weeding his vast garden full of Jerusalem artichokes and other exotic vegetables. As I was eight-months pregnant, I couldn't bend over easily and found myself crawling with my trowel between the garden rows.

In the fall of 1964, we moved to Cambridge into Apartment F-21-S in Peabody Terrace, a new apartment complex on the Charles River, designed by Jean Luis Sert and built for Harvard graduate students, who at the time were mostly men, and their families.

Katrina Anne Sorenson was born on September 25, 1964. A year later, on October 23, 1965, also at the Boston Lying-in Hospital, our son Eric Ripley Sorenson was born. My birthing experience in Boston was so different from what I had experienced in Switzerland that I wrote to the hospital management describing the differences and suggesting some changes. The administrators replied, assuring me that they welcomed and would institute my recommendations, at least some of them. Once again, even though I was not pampered as I had been in La Clinique des Charmettes in Lausanne, it felt to me as though trillions of stars shone more brightly on the nights when Katrina and Eric were born; birds chorused in exquisite harmony at dawn and bright fall leaves fluttered to the ground and covered it like a brilliant tapestry. I was filled with joy. I loved and will always love my three children with my whole heart. Someday, I will write a book about each of them. Each one is unique and special with wonderful distinctive qualities that have been evident since birth.

Bud and I were elated to be back in Cambridge, my hometown, with its bookstores and cafés. In the spring, summer, and fall, I relished walking along the Charles River pushing a stroller with my three beautiful, amazing children. Bud could easily walk across the river to his doctoral student office at HBS.

We made many friends while living in Peabody Terrace, helping each other with baby-sitting and advice. I did find, however, that with three children under three, two in cloth diapers with rusty safety pins, and no help with childcare, housework, shopping, or cooking, I was constantly exhausted. It was especially difficult when, just a month after Trina's birth, Bud spent six weeks (October 29–December 15, 1964) in Central America gathering information for his doctoral thesis. We had no phone contact during that time. I poured out my heart in letters each day and mailed them to general USAID post boxes in Guatemala and El Salvador.

In one letter, I described a recent visit to my gynecologist, Chief of Gynecology at a major Boston hospital. I told Bud only that I had seen the doctor for a check-up. I didn't tell him that the doctor was alone with me in the examining room and had said inappropriate and suggestive things that confused and scared me. Only in the past year, free to speak out because of the #MeToo movement, did I recount this incident to my daughters and Bud. If this were to happen to me today, I would run out of the examining room and immediately report what I had felt to have been alarming behavior to everyone in the waiting room. At the time, however, over fifty years ago, I probably thanked the doctor politely and quietly left the office. I never returned to that doctor, but I also never reported his behavior to hospital authorities. I was so shaken by my experience that I got lost driving the short, familiar route back to Cambridge.

Perhaps, because of that incident, I wrote to Bud: "*I begin to see that life is big and deep and real and sort of scary. Trying to understand it and maneuver through it takes a lot of courage.*" That is true. Today, I would add that life also takes among many other things, a sense of humor and a certain detachment, an ability to see one's life as ultimately inconsequential in the grand, cosmic scheme of things.

In 1966, Bud received his doctorate and joined the HBS faculty as an Assistant Professor. His first assignment was as the head of the Harvard University Advisory Group in the Philippines. Based in Manila and funded by the Ford Foundation, the mission of this project was to help develop full-time graduate MBA programs for three Filipino academic institutions: Ateneo de Manila University, a private Jesuit university, De la Salle College, run by the Christian Brothers, and the University of the Philippines.

I was proud of Bud for taking on this challenge. Personally, I looked forward to this re-location in the Philippines both as a new experience as well as salvation from my state of nervous exhaustion from caring for three small children. I had heard that we would have household help.

Chapter Six

Life in the Philippines

and Travels in Asia (1966–1968)

From an early age, even before living in Switzerland, European countries formed part of my mental landscape. That was true, I believe, for anyone brought up in New England, the destination of European immigrants and trade from earliest times. For Easterners, ours was a Greco-Roman heritage. My art history classes at Wellesley had reflected that bias, concentrating almost solely on European art.

Although I could identify major Asian countries on a map, I knew next to nothing about each county's unique culture, its economy or politics. We were going to live in the Philippines, an archipelago of 7,641 islands located between the South China Sea and the Pacific Ocean. I was excited at the thought that I had so much to explore and to learn. I was twenty-six years old.

It was an endless flight from Boston across the Pacific to Manila with three young children. We stopped three times to re-fuel, in San Francisco, Hawaii, and Guam. Eric astounded passengers and crew by standing in his bulkhead bassinette for the better part of ten hours crowing and waving. Trina ate most of the candy in the lounge and Kristin wrote her name endlessly and drew thatched-roofed nipa huts for the crew. The small white pills from the doctor that were supposed to put them to sleep did not work.

Descending toward Manila over the main island of Luzon, we saw a rugged coastline, several cone-shaped mountains, and a verdant, tropical countryside. Closer to Manila, we could see small villages, rice fields, and water buffalo. Fishermen in outrigger canoes populated the rivers.

Upon landing, we were met by some of our friends in the Harvard Advisory Group and by intense heat and humidity. As we stepped from the plane, the steward murmured, "Prepare yourselves." It was the rainy season in the Philippines and there had just been two days of typhoon rains. The water was waist high in the main streets of downtown Manila which is below sea level. Cars were stalled in the gutted pavements, buses and *jeepneys* had lost their wheels. In many of the small outdoor restaurants, water came up to the bottom of the benches. We saw people swimming out of the shacks where they lived and drinking Coca-Cola in the waterlogged restaurants. Seeing this as we were driven to our home, I realized that we had been met, not only by heat and humidity, but also by extreme poverty.

Our Ford Foundation-furnished home at 22 Tolentino Street was located in San Lorenzo Village, a neighborhood compound in Makati, Metro Manila. The compound was surrounded by a concrete wall topped with barbed wire and broken glass. The gates were locked and guarded. Armed guards, we were told, rode through the streets on bicycles day and night. It bothered me enormously to think that we would have to live this way, acting as though the Filipinos were by nature and design criminals, as if we would have to be constantly on our guard against theft and deceit. It was not the American way nor was it, for that matter, the Swiss way. We flinched at the way the rich and the poor were completely segregated. There was clearly no middle class. It was not until a few weeks had passed that we began to understand that our children's health and safety and our own peace of mind would depend upon accepting this way of life. In addition, the tropical climate was enervating. It was clear that one would collapse without access to a cool retreat.

Our house was modern and spacious with air-conditioned bedrooms. Gloria, the children's gentle and loving *ya-ya* (or nanny) and Tina, the kind *lavandera* (or laundress) met us at the door and immediately took the children to bathe them and put them to bed. I had never been more grateful for help. In my bedroom, I spent a few moments watching the geckos, small unblinking lizards, crawling up the walls, clicking and chirping. Then I fell onto the bed and slept for twelve hours.

I wrote regularly to my parents about our life in the Philippines. They especially wanted to hear about their grandchildren. I include some of those letters here:

> Eric, eight months old, has never been happier. I don't know what spending the day in the arms of one's ya-ya does to a boy's sense of independence, but he is delighted, gurgles and crows and watches the fan in the living room whirl round and round. Maybe he will be a philosopher. Trina was a bit leery of the new situation at first, seeing me disappear into the air-conditioned bedroom with her father to talk when he came home at night or leaving for a walk with Gloria when Bud and I were sitting plain as day at the breakfast table. Kristin sang, "Happy Days are

Here Again" during the entire first day. By great good luck, she was placed in the kindergarten of the neighborhood school, so she already has friends.

Shortly after our arrival, I took Trina to a Chinese birthday party. There were forty two-year-olds, thirty-nine ya-yas and one out-of-place American mother who had forgotten to bring a ya-ya. I was left standing on the lawn pushing Trina on the swing while all of the other mothers had gone inside to escape the heat. The next day at a Filipino birthday party, I took two helpers!

The Harvard Advisory Group was enthusiastically welcomed. All of the Filipinos whom we met were friendly and hospitable. When we first arrived, there was much discussion within the Advisory Group of the need for an educated managerial class, a group that could grasp the specific needs of the Filipino people. This would mean training Filipinos, not Americans, to solve Filipino problems.

We heard many stories of the atrocities and cruelty of the Japanese in the Philippines during World War II. The war in the Pacific had ended just twenty years earlier. One of our close friends watched, hidden under the porch of her house, as Japanese soldiers raped her mother and then brutally murdered both her mother and her father. We learned about the Japanese siege of the island of Corregidor in Manila Bay and about the Bataan Death March in 1942 during which 10,000 Allied and Filipino soldiers died. The prisoners were forced to march in intense tropical heat and horrific conditions for sixty-five miles. They were given starvation rations during the eight-day march and were beaten, stabbed, and shot at random by the Japanese. The Bataan Death March was later considered by the Allied Military Commission to be a Japanese war crime.

One evening, we had dinner with four American boys who were fighting in Vietnam. They talked of fire ants and grenades and wondered why they were there and what they were fighting for. We had no answers. Just as the troubles in Cuba had seemed far away when we lived in Switzerland, the war in Vietnam seemed distant to us, even though Vietnam and the Philippines are close geographically. Vowing to fight the spread of Communism, President Lyndon Johnson had sent the first American combat troops to Vietnam the previous year, in March 1965, a year before our arrival in the Philippines. We began to hear of anti-war demonstrations at home.

How did we spend our evenings? A few months after our arrival, I wrote:

> Our life here has been hectic. There is literally a party each night. I thought that you might be interested in where and with whom, so here is a list:
>
> On December 1, there was a gathering of HBS alumni, then dinner with a Filipino-Chilean couple, our friends Bobby and Monica Ongpin, followed the next night by dinner with friends to talk about traveling through Asia in a Land Rover. One couple had done it; the other wanted to. The next night dancing, learning *tininkling*, the national dance. This is a potential ankle-breaker. It consists of hopping to fast music between two bamboo poles that are held at the ends, then clacked together in a rhythm.
>
> Then, a birthday party for a member of the Harvard

Advisory Group. This was interesting, as there were several anthropologists present. Catherine Bateson, the wife of one of the members of the Harvard Advisory Group, is Margaret Mead's daughter. Upon arriving in the Philippines, Catherine, a linguist in her own right, began studying Tagalog. Even though more than 170 languages are spoken on the 7,641 islands that comprise the Philippine archipelago, English and Tagalog are the country's two official languages.

The next evening, there was a reception at the magnificent home of Washington Sycip, a supporter of the work of the Harvard Advisory Group. Wash is a Chinese-Filipino, a population that is resented by many Filipinos, as Chinese-Filipinos control most of the banks and large businesses as well as the small *sari-sari* (general) stores. After dinner, the women and the men were briskly and irrevocably separated for coffee and I suppose, for the men, cigars. In the room where coffee was served to the beautifully dressed, coiffed, and manicured ladies, the snapping of fans was impressive.

The following afternoon, we spent with friends playing mahjong at an elaborate nipa hut on a bluff overlooking Manila. Then, there was a reception in a Spanish villa for Steve Fuller, the HBS professor who had set up the Philippine project. Then, another reception for Steve with sixty guests at our house. Then, dinner with the Rufinos', then, a stag affair—whew—then, a Christmas party at one of the three universities involved in the project, then, then, then . . .

We are meeting a variety of people, in business, government, and the arts. I recently met a Chinese brush painter who told me about an experience at the University of the Philippines where he had been demonstrating brush-painting.

He had the feeling that four radical students had purposely posted themselves at the four corners of the hall. They fired questions at him about the Cultural Revolution and Chairman Mao Zedong who since last May has been terrorizing the Chinese educated class. The artist was a quiet, sensitive man who was unnerved by the barbed, sarcastic questions. His hand shook, and he had to stop his demonstration.

Perhaps the liveliest of our new friends are the Jesuit Fathers from Ateneo de Manila, the Harvard of the Philippines, and the Christian Brothers from De La Salle. Father James Donelan, the President of Ateneo is my favorite. He is a scholar and a humanist who gives talks on the Renaissance and the Enlightenment.

In all of the lovely gardens and homes that we visit, the air is scented with the fragrance of frangipani, oleander, tuberoses, and night-flowering jasmine. Bougainvillea, hibiscus and epiphytes like orchids bloom everywhere in this moist tropical atmosphere.

The warmth and hospitality of the Filipinos whom we have met is extraordinary and seductive. The parties are extravagant, sometimes ostentatious. Because I enjoy the easy hospitality and the merriment, I sometimes feel vaguely guilty as if somewhere on the International Date Line, while traveling to the Philippines, I may have dropped the familiar Yankee mantras of restraint, modesty, frugality, self-discipline, independence, diligence and hard work. It will be a trick to keep from being spoiled.

It is all breathtaking, exhausting, and entertaining. However, one wonders how the Filipinos get their business done and keep the government operating. This way of life, travel, is totally dependent upon the household help that everyone has. A whirlwind social life notwithstanding, Kristin, Trina and Eric are my highest priority. I never leave the house until I am sure that I have listened to, talked with, and read to each of them and made sure that they are safe, well cared for, and happy.

We kept learning new things about the Philippines. It is a Catholic country, the Catholic faith having been brought to the islands by the Spanish who controlled the country for about 350 years, from 1521 to 1898 A.D. The name *de la Cruz* was a popular surname. It means "of the Cross" and was the family name given to the bastard children of the lonely Spanish Catholic priests. The name *de los Reyes* was another popular surname given to the bastard children of the probably equally lonely magistrates who had been sent by the Spanish king to govern this distant island nation.

We learned, too, how English became the *lingua franca* of the Philippines. After the Americans defeated the Spanish in 1898 in the Spanish-American War, the U.S. government in 1901 sent 500 American teachers to the Philippines on the U.S.S. *Thomas* to "civilize and educate" the Filipinos. Called *Thomasites*, they fanned out over the islands teaching English to the island inhabitants. They taught American English with books that featured snow and apple trees. Fluency in English has given the Philippines an advantage in certain political and economic respects, as it is one of the few English-speaking countries in Asia.

For Bud, the days were full of meetings, teaching, seminars, and traveling the rutted roads between the three schools trying to think through the best strategy for improving their management programs. He did have a driver. According to all reports, he was doing a marvelous job. I was so proud of him.

My life, in turn, consisted of running the household, taking care of children with fevers and coughs, participating in required social events, and learning the ups and downs of life in a tropical country. I had much to learn about managing a household which, besides the cook, the ya-ya and the lavandera, also included a gardener, a seamstress who came every two weeks to sew clothes for the children, and a part-time driver. Rosa, our betel-nut chewing, black-toothed cook, went twice a week to *Divisoria*, the extensive local market to shop for papayas, mangoes, calamansi (like a lime, but milder in flavor), coconuts, pineapples, rice, chicken, pork, and fish. We ate lots of rice, often in a popular dish called chicken adobo. In addition to its being a food market, we learned that most of the goods, besides the foodstuff, that were for sale in Divisoria were either imported or smuggled. Eventually, I had to fire Rosa for stealing, rather pilfering. This resulted in my having to set up a tighter system of controls on food and supplies. I did not like having to be more watchful with regard to the help.

Our first Philippine Christmas, December 1966:

> It's just a week before Christmas and, although there is a typhoon with a Tagalog name raging outside, we are full of nostalgia and warm feelings for the Berkshires and crisp weather and greens and home. People here sing about a white Christmas and about dashing through the snow, but it is hopelessly unrealistic. We made our own tree, attaching ordinary garden brooms made of twigs to a bamboo pole. We fabricated a brick fireplace out of a table and a wall and

red paper, so that we will have a place to hang stockings. Hidden in a closet is a magnificent horse made of papier-mâché painted in bright reds, greens and yellows like a traditional Swedish horse. It is mounted on a red platform with wheels. This will give Gloria and the children great pleasure as she wheels them around the neighborhood. We have erected a small bamboo and thatched-roof nipa hut in the front yard for the children to use as a playhouse.

Kristin was in very good voice at her school holiday program, lustily singing "Joy to the World" and "Angels We Have Heard on High," especially, thinking of her ya-ya, in the "Gloria" chorus. She participates enthusiastically in whatever is happening, helping others and offering wise advice. She writes and draws constantly. She pressed one of her dresses in secret today. She was embarrassed to confess to Tina that she had scorched it.

Trina continues to be a white-haired dervish. She can be seen at almost any hour of the day running from the kitchen to her room, hot on the trail of *Pusa*, her cat. When at long last she corners the cat, she picks it up and walks nonchalantly about the house in search of new and better adventures. Gloria found her recently walking down Tolentino Street, dragging a wicker cage holding a rice bird. She has two new ducklings.

Eric, at one year and two months of age, displays flashes of physical and mental brilliance. Gloria can't get over his prodigious feats of strength at the playground. "He is so strong, Ma'am." Eric is amiable and kind. I am trying to organize a small play school for him here at the house, so that he won't indulge himself all day in the attentions and arms of the maids.

Taking Gloria with us to watch after Eric, we left on the day after Christmas for the mountain town of Baguio, five hours by car north of Manila. It was a glorious four days in the cool, crisp, pine-scented mountain air with ponies for the children to ride and with pigs, goats, chickens and a horse near our small house that was isolated on a hillside. During the evenings, we entertained friends with songs, games, and cheese fondue by the fire.

Initially, the Philippines seemed Westernized to us, yet beneath this familiar veneer were cultural layers and undercurrents rooted in its Malay, Spanish and Muslim history. There was so much to understand. I doubted whether a visitor from the West could even begin to grasp the complicated feelings that Filipinos have towards themselves, their families and their culture. In terms of population, the Philippines is diverse. In the northern mountains of the main island of Luzon, for example, head-hunting by the Illongot tribe was practiced until it was outlawed by the Americans in the 1930s. In the southern islands, Islam has been an established religion since the fourteenth century.

I began to read news articles about American middle-class women, ex-patriots living in the Philippines, who, suddenly blessed with domestic help and leisure time, quickly adopted the lifestyles of the rich. There was truth to this observation, I thought. It would be tempting and easy to turn into a colonialist. I tried to figure out how I could be of service or make a contribution in this culture. One evening at a function at the American Embassy, I met Joan Wilson, the wife of the American Ambassador, James M. Wilson. She asked if I would be interested in working with her to start a cooperative pre-school in Manila. Without hesitation, I said yes.

In fact, I had brought some ideas and materials from Cambridge just in case I might have an opportunity to develop a pre-school program in Manila.

We started working the next day planning for the school. We called it the International Cooperative Pre-school. The Union Church in Makati gave us permission to house the pre-school in its basement. We soon received all of the necessary city permits. We determined the educational criteria for the school, selected the teachers, helped plan the program, and opened the enrollment. We immediately attracted mothers and children from the international community. We hoped to attract Filipino children and their mothers as well. The school was non-denominational and welcomed children from all nations.

The school was obviously needed. After only two months, the International Cooperative Pre-school was operating at full tilt with forty three and four-year-old children and two excellent teachers. Its enrollment, however, was ninety-five percent American. That was our major concern. We wanted to get more Filipinas involved. We thought that would happen once the school was a recognized success. We assumed that we could persuade Filipina mothers to come to the school with their children and read to them and assist the teachers. That was difficult. Volunteering was a familiar concept in America, but not in the Philippines.

Later and out of the blue, I received a letter of recommendation from Joan Wilson. I was truly grateful for her kind words and support. I passed her letter on to my family:

> *I asked Mrs. Sorenson to help me establish a cooperative nursery school because of her demonstrated interest in creating a school to meet a specific need in the international community. We worked together very closely determining educational*

criteria for the school, planning the program, selecting teachers and jointly supervising the first year of operation.

Mrs. Sorenson is one of the most gifted young women with whom I have worked in many years of cooperative school activity and volunteer welfare operations in the United States and overseas. She works with children in a quiet but consistent manner, showing deep, almost compassionate interest in the individual child and demonstrating a quality of serenity along with a flair for organization. She has high intelligence, poise, warmth of personality and a firm sense of purpose. She will always be an outstanding performer in any endeavor she undertakes, but it is very pleasing to me and to others who have worked with her in Manila to know that her interest in education is foremost, for she has a true gift for teaching. Her fellow teachers at the American School commented to me on Mrs. Sorenson's impressive qualities as a teacher and a friend.

One morning I woke up feeling deflated and sad. The day before I had exploded at our second cook because I thought she was using too much sugar. A small thing, indeed! It turned out that I was wrong, and she was right. She told Bud that she was an honest woman, that she had never been treated like this before and that she was going to quit. The thing that really bothered me was that I questioned her to her face without really being sure of the facts, that I challenged her integrity without reason. That was a serious offense. For the Filipinos, in fact, for all Asians, saving face is of the utmost importance. I gave her no way out except to quit. I felt terrible about offending her and about being such an inept, insensitive manager. I resolved to do better.

If we had known that the waters of the Lingayan Gulf contained unexploded mines and deadly poisonous fish, we might have reconsidered our plan to camp out on an island there. The Hundred Islands, 124 of them, are ancient coral atolls shaped like mushroom caps. In our planning, we also did not consider the tides. At high tide, the tiny necklace of sand at the base of the mushroom stem would likely be covered with water, leaving little room for camping.

Knowing nothing about these matters, we left Manila in February in high spirits with a hamper of fruit, a roast chicken, water and wine, and with our friends Monica and Bobby Ongpin. It took us seven hours to drive 109 miles over medium-bad and very-bad bumpy, rutted roads to northwestern Luzon to a nameless, ramshackle fishing village. At that time, the Hundred Islands had no hotels. It was not a tourist destination. We hired a fisherman who said he would take us in his outrigger canoe to an island, leave us there for a few days and nights, then come to collect us.

We found an island, determined that the high tide did not completely cover the sand, and spread our straw mats and sleeping bags as close to the base of the stem as we could. During the afternoon, we read and snorkeled. We laid out our chicken supper on a rock. The tide was rising as we dined, the seawater swirling around our ankles. In the evening, we lay on our woven mats hoping that our tidal calculation was accurate. Under a full moon, we sang, told stories and studied the constellations. The sea was brilliant with phosphorescence.

The following day, we collected shells for our children and lay on the sand watching the antics of the squatter crabs, the small crabs that eat the inhabitants of a particularly desirable shell. Having eaten the owner, the robbers then crawl into their new acquisitions and strut about showing off. Sometimes the new shell homes are massive and heavy, crab McMansions. The greedy, arrogant crabs begin to totter, then to stagger as they wander down the sand. Humbled. Time to downsize. I watched them for hours. Not all of the crabs were greedy, though. Sometimes, the new shells fit perfectly.

The water looked fine. Bud went swimming far out into the sea. He came back holding what looked like an unexploded naval mine, wires sticking out of the ordnance in all directions. The Lingayan Gulf on the main island of Luzon, we remembered, had been the scene of a major battle in World War II. On January 9, 1945, under attack by the suicidal Japanese kamikaze pilots whose last words were "Long Live the Emperor," General Douglas MacArthur, had successfully stormed the beach in an amphibious landing.

After the success of this battle, MacArthur continued his campaign to re-take the Philippines. The Battle of Manila was violent, resulting in the ultimate surrender of the Japanese. The battle was described in detail by our friend Marcial Lichauco, a lawyer and diplomat, in his book, published in 1949, *Dear Mother Putnam: Life and Death in Manila During the Japanese Occupation.* Marcial had been the first Filipino accepted at Harvard College.

World War II in the Pacific ended on September 2, 1945, four months after Germany surrendered to the Allies on May 7, 1945. General MacArthur met Hirohito, the Japanese Emperor. What was the etiquette? Should he bow or shake hands? Hirohito, MacArthur knew, was not only the Emperor of Japan. In the eyes of the Japanese, he was also a God.

In our excitement imagining the battles of Lingayan Gulf and Manila, we failed to notice that the time had long passed for the outrigger canoe to return to collect us. The tide was rising and worse, we had run out of food. Bud, ever resourceful, put the chicken bones from last night's dinner into our only pot, filled it with sea water, heated it and voilà! a savory chicken broth. Just at that moment, just in time, before a sure-to-be fatal sip, the outrigger canoe appeared on the horizon.

On the drive back to Manila, we passed cart after cart on their way to market, festooned with baskets of all sizes and shapes. We drove slowly through small barrios. Children played on clean-swept dirt underneath nipa huts built on tall stilts. Older women walked with huge baskets on their heads smoking cigars or chewing betel nuts. Small girls carried their infant siblings. Grizzled old men stroked their prized fighting cocks or crouched beside their huts in groups of four, gambling, tossing coins into the center of a circle they had etched in the dirt. They all had jet black hair and black eyes and were very loving with their children. In one village, an old man wandered down the street with a basket calling out, "*Balut, Balut.*" A Philippine delicacy and supposed aphrodisiac, *Balut* is a fertilized duck embryo, boiled and eaten from the shell. Whether it has feathers and a beak depends upon how long it has gestated.

On another trip, we visited IRRI, the International Rice Research Institute in Los Banos, south of Manila. The agronomists there were trying to perfect a miracle rice that would withstand pests and climate challenges. The new rice was not popular, however, as, in the opinion of the Filipinos, it had a strange taste and consistency and, above all, a strange smell. I hadn't realized that rice has an odor, but Dr. Chandler, the head of the Institute, assured us that smell is one of the most important criteria for the villagers to consider as they select rice for their families.

Dr. Chandler led us on a hike up a nearby mountain. It was a rough climb in the tropical heat through a dense rain forest.

Sometimes we had to hack our way using sharp, machete-like bolos. When we came down from the mountain, my legs were covered with black leeches that I had to burn off with lighted cigarettes.

In a nearby province, we shot the rapids in a canoe at Pagsanjian Falls, monkeys chattering overhead, jade vines (celadon-green orchids) garlanding the cliffs. Water cascades 400 feet in the main waterfall. Bud, standing under the powerful falls, lost his wedding ring. Again, like the Hundred Islands, Pagsanjian Falls was not a tourist attraction. We were the only people there.

Once, we traveled by private plane to the southern tip of the main island of Luzon where we met our host and the skipper of a small boat. We cruised for four days, fishing, snorkeling, collecting shells, sleeping under the stars on the front deck. We were watched over constantly in all of these activities by the bodyguard of our host. Armed with a 22-caliber pistol, the bodyguard would precede us to a deserted beach, scan it nervously, then settle in the shade of a palm tree. Japanese soldiers were said to be hiding in the jungles of remote islands, refusing to surrender even twenty years after the defeat of the Japanese army in 1945. They were still loyal to the Emperor.

Skinny, weathered fishermen came in their *bancas* to the side of our boat with baskets of fresh fish. I stepped during that trip on a venomous sea urchin and was told to urinate on the bottom of my foot to dissolve the alkaline spine. Challenging! On a remote beach wearing heavy leather gloves, we collected sea urchins with spines six inches long, opened them, flavored them with a little lemon juice and ate the delicate, buttery insides. Sea urchins or *oursins* are considered a great delicacy in France.

At one point, I spent six days in Hong Kong with three friends. The city is an emporium, a shopper's paradise. I was dazzled by the pearls, the jade, the silks, the spices, the English woolens.

I didn't buy much, but I bargained at all of the stalls and was tempted by everything. The Chinese are highly organized and competitive, sober and restrained in their attitude toward life and very disciplined. I was grateful that they demonstrated these characteristics in our small transactions, but I missed Manila's gaiety and zest. Nobody smiled in Hong Kong. By contrast, the Filipinos smiled easily and constantly.

In the spring of 1967, we started pouring over guide books and maps planning our six-week home leave. We planned to go around the world with our three young children, ages five, three, and two. We wanted to travel to Bangkok to meditate in front of the Golden Buddha, to Rangoon in Burma, to Agra in India to be astounded by the beauty of the Taj Mahal, to Srinigar in Kashmir where we had already rented a houseboat, to Athens to climb the Acropolis, then to Vienna to have tea with the Guschlbauers, to Switzerland where we had rented an apartment for a week in a chateau above Lake Geneva, and finally home, to Stockbridge and Pilgrims Inn.

We tried to calculate the number of minutes it would take to get the stroller and our jugs of boiled water, the bag of diapers and snacks and stomach medications and three small children from plane to temple, to the Taj Mahal, to the houseboat, to the fabled Gardens of Shalimar, to Vienna for tea with the Guschlbauers, to the chateau in Switzerland, and then across the Atlantic without missing any planes or losing any children

Chapter Seven

Around the World

and Back to Manila
(July 1967)

Our flight to Srinigar in Kashmir was epic. We arrived in Delhi from the Philippines at two in the morning. The main hall of the airport was cavernous and brutally hot. Wooden fans swirled overhead. People in rags were sleeping along the edges of the room. Bud confirmed that our flight to Srinigar was scheduled to leave at 5:30 that morning. We took a taxi to a simple rest house nearby. At least we could rest for three hours.

Back at the airport by five, we were informed by the airline agent that the plane had already left. "But, but," stuttered Bud. "We stood here and reconfirmed just three hours ago."

"So sorry, sir, but the plane filled up and the pilot decided to take off."

Upstairs, the airport restaurant was open to the sky. A few bamboo poles placed horizontally above the edge of the restaurant floor were supposed to keep people from falling to the tarmac below. We spent the day there, drinking Cokes and eating hard-boiled eggs and dry toast. Anything else was guaranteed to cause dysentery.

Finally, about five in the afternoon, we were informed that we could board our plane. We were seated in a row of three seats (all five of us) just behind the bulkhead. I write, "we were seated," when, in fact, the moment we sat down, the seats rocked forward and fell out of their sockets. The three seats across the aisle from us were empty.

The temperature in the plane must have been well over 130 degrees, as it had been sitting on the tarmac closed up all day under the tropical sun. The stewardess offered us water. Deadly, we thought, and declined, even though our children were panting and reaching out for the glasses.

We were about to take off. "Please fasten your seat belts." At that moment, a surge of seven children and their mother settled on the three seats opposite ours. "Oh, yes, sir. It's fine, sir. She is the wife of the pilot, sir. That is his family, sir."

We flew over the Himalayas and into the fabled Vale of Kashmir. Upon landing, the door of the plane opened, and we were greeted by air that was clear, cool, and scented. Kashmir is indeed an earthly paradise. For a week, we stayed in Srinigar on the Jhelum River in a carved wooden houseboat, the *Merry Dawn*. Each morning, small wooden boats, *shikaras*, floated by with merchants selling hand-woven Kashmiri shawls and rugs, walnuts and pomegranates, bags of lapis lazuli and other semi-precious stones. It was hard to keep our fascinated children from falling overboard into the fast-flowing river. On land near the stern of the boat, the captain, Gulfar, baked the most astonishing walnut soufflés over an open fire and told us his story. His had been an arranged marriage. He had not seen the bride until he was allowed to lift her veil on their wedding day. What he saw did not please him and he fled that day to Australia where he lived for sixteen years serving an Englishman as his *batman* or personal servant.

We made an excursion by local bus to Gulmarg, a mountainous area of open alpine meadows. There were no hotels or ski lifts at that time, only a few men on horseback gathered in a group, gesticulating and shouting about some local matter.

We visited the Mughal Gardens of Shalimar, built in 1619 by the Mughal Emperor Jahangir for his beloved wife, Nur Jahan, Light of the World. We strolled past family groups of Hindus who were spending the day picnicking and smoking hookahs and Muslims who had spread their prayer rugs and were praying at the appointed hours. Exploring on her own, Trina tripped suddenly and fell into one of the clear Shalimar pools. She was rescued in an instant by Bud and adopted immediately by a hospitable Hindu family who had enjoyed the spectacle.

At the end of our stay, in an effort to return to Delhi, we took a taxi for three mornings in a row from the houseboat to the Srinigar airport. Each morning, we were told that it would be too dangerous to fly over the Himalayas whose massive peaks were hidden in thick clouds. Then, on the third morning, sitting in our taxi, we watched a few Air India planes streak down through a hole in the clouds and land. We were told to leave our taxi immediately and run as fast as we could toward the planes. We had only a few minutes before they would take off again. We made it, sank into seats that didn't fall out of their sockets, and hung on as we shot almost straight up out of beautiful Kashmir, up through the hole in the clouds, up, up and finally up and over the Himalayas.

On the banks of the Danube, the early spring sun twinkled through the fresh new leaves. The air was cool. The river sparkled. Birds sang. According to plan, Herr und Frau Guschlbauer picked us up at the airport in Vienna and took us to a small fish restaurant beside the Danube, the first to open that spring. Our rendez-vous over fish fillets was filled with warmth and laughter. That brief but unforgettable lunch taught me the importance of cherishing each one of life's moments, each moment, each smile or word having the potential to turn into a glowing memory or perhaps a life-changing event.

When I think of that short visit, it reminds me of a few lines by an unknown author that I memorized long ago:

> *"We live among pilgrims. Each encounter with another is an exchange of gifts to be carried homeward. May we give singing in the soul."*

In just a few hours, the Guschlbauers with their kindness and generosity had given us *singing in the soul*, that special gift, before whisking us back to the airport to catch our flight to Switzerland, the next stop on our amazing trip around the world.

After a few days visiting with old friends in Lausanne, we spent a few weeks at Pilgrims Inn and with Bud's family in Ohio.

Returning to the Philippines, we made a brief stop in Japan. There, we slept on tatami mats for a few days in a Japanese inn in Kyoto and visited the breath-taking Silver and Gold Pavilions and serene temples and gardens. We purchased a stunning red *tonsu* (chest) that we carried with us on the plane to Manila. A few days in Kyoto, Taiwan and Hong Kong, then racing to catch the plane, loaded with seventeen, yes, seventeen pieces of hand luggage. We gave two to Kristin to carry and Bud and I somehow carried the rest. I truly don't know how we managed to convey the impression that the leaden bags that we were carrying were light. Smiling, we insisted, "Oh, no thanks, never mind, they are light. Well, if you could carry the baby?"

I knew instantly when we stepped out of the airport late at night that we were back in Manila. The steamy air had a distinctive odor, a combination of brine and fish and seaweed, outdoor fires, food cooked in hot oil and fish paste mixed with the strong fragrance of oleander, frangipani and pollution. After our trip, I thanked my parents for their Homeric hospitality during our stay at Pilgrims Inn and reported on our arrival back in Manila:

> Trina and Eric are just back from a walk, Eric with his wide blue eyes, soft blond hair and a happy smile toddling as fast as he can after Gloria. Trina is in her nothings, babbling away cheerfully about all of the fine and wonderful birds and airplanes and flowers and dogs and cats that she saw on their walk, her babblings accompanied with vast gestures and fallings-down and leapings-up to illustrate her tale. She likes to crawl around on the floor after her new turtle. Three ducks and two ricebirds have all been lovingly buried during our stay. Let us hope that the turtle hides under its shell and survives.
>
> Kristin is up on the ladder that leans against the high wall separating us from our neighbor. In a loud voice, she informs me that the next-door lavandera is using Clorox on a blue dress, which she shouldn't do, because the dress will turn white. Continuing in a loud voice, Kristin announces that she likes maids, that living here is like living in a hotel, that maids do everything for you, while in America mothers have to do all of the work . . .
>
> I think this will be a wonderful year. The children are well cared for by Gloria and Tina. We have good friends. Bud's work is absorbing and useful. The household is running smoothly with our new cook, Freddie, in charge. Returning from our six-week trip actually felt like coming home.

Kristin just came running into our living room shouting, "I can read!" She was looking at books last night before falling asleep and lo and behold! It happened! New worlds will open up that she can explore for a lifetime.

Eric is at the window singing "Rain, rain, go away." But it doesn't, so he keeps on singing.

We were inundated with activities immediately upon returning from our six-week home leave. I began teaching at the American School, a kindergarten class of twenty children. The hours were from 7 am to noon. I had Jose in my class who muttered all the time, "Oh, let the maids do it!" Little Mike, built like a tank and missing his two front teeth, would hide under the table and kiss my hand whenever I entered or left the room. James sighed endlessly as if the world was really too much. There was well-adjusted Becky, flirtatious Heidi, Pastoral Paul and lovely, charming, communicative, organized Ling-Ling who reminded me of Kristin. I was relieved that Josh, potentially a problem student, had been moved to another class. Jose, though, still shrugged and snarled and hated almost everyone.

I finished teaching just in time to pick up Kristin from first grade. She was suffering. The discipline in her class was distinctly different from anything she had ever known. Sitting still for hours at desks. No talking. Raising hands before speaking. Endless recitation of the ABC's. Silence during juice time. Books to carry home and homework every night.

Bud sailed right into all sorts of problems to be solved, people to meet, and issues to deal with as he worked with the three schools to figure out their futures. He was now deeply involved in an optimistic attempt to merge the management schools of the two Catholic academic institutions involved in the program, Ateneo de Manila and De la Salle.

In September, Professor Steve Fuller spent a week in Manila. He was a dynamic man with the sensitivities and energy of a politician. I was fascinated to see how he flattered and soothed and cajoled and suggested and, in general, operated. Within five minutes one night as I listened, he decimated one man's chances to succeed with a certain project and at the same time gave the green light to another man's chances at HBS. Influence equals power. Fortunately, as far as we knew, Bud had Steve's support. We heard that this project, from the point of view of the Ford Foundation, had taken off faster and progressed more quickly than any project they had ever sponsored. Steve wanted Bud to stay on for another year.

One day for fun, we went to a beach, dressed our naked children in seaweed, like mermaids and mermen, covered each one in sand, then ran in the rain and jumped in the surf. A large crowd of Filipino children gathered to watch, silent and staring with large black eyes, fascinated in particular by Trina's white hair.

Another day, we went on an excursion with Delly Bautista, one of my co-teachers at the American School. We visited some archaeological digs somewhere south of Manila where the archaeologists had been excited to find Chinese trade ware from the twelfth and thirteenth centuries.

We also visited the home of Jose Rizal, a Philippine National Hero. Rizal was a doctor, poet and journalist who fought for freedom from the 350 years of Spanish colonial rule. Using the force and persuasiveness of his writings, he urged a peaceful revolution. At the age of thirty-five on December 30, 1896, he was executed as a revolutionary by a Spanish firing squad. His book, *Noli Me Tangere (Don't Touch Me)* describes the hypocrisy of the Spanish Catholic priests and the cruelty of the Spanish colonial government.

Two quotes from the works of Jose Rizal:

> *"There can be no tyrants where there are no slaves."*

> *"It is a useless life if not consecrated to a great ideal. It is like a stone wasted on the field without becoming a part of an edifice."*

The presidential election in the fall of 1967 was hard-fought and bloody. President Ferdinand Marcos got all of his *Nacionalistas* into power. We wondered what positive things he would be able to do with them. Marcos was considered at the time to be an intelligent, thoughtful, and progressive president.

Prime Minister Sato of Japan visited the Philippines during the fall. It was interesting to see the reaction of the Filipinos. Their ambivalent feelings were summed up in the bold headline in the *Manila Times*, "We Can Forgive, But We Can Never Forget." The irony was that Japan, the vanquished, had grown to be the strongest, wealthiest nation in Asia. In contrast, the Filipinos were now very much in need of economic aid and assistance from Japan.

We kept reading with shock and bewilderment about the riots and anti-war demonstrations in the U.S. There seemed to be so many lies coming out of Washington. We could only hope and pray that this violence would be just a temporary phase in the fight for civil rights in America and for the end of the war in Vietnam.

Our second Christmas in the Philippines:

> Our wicker tree is up, hung with glowing capiz shells and wooden cherries and a bird's nest holding golden eggs perched on one of the curlicued wicker branches. Holding

a tilting platter, Eric is toddling around smiling and passing juice, sardines and pizza to the family.

Santa Claus is actually coming to our house on Christmas Eve. Don't tell anyone. Enormous Brother Hyacinth Gabriel, President of de la Salle College, has consented to come dressed in red (I provided the cloth) with a white beard. (I provided the cotton.) He will carry a sack with toys that I purchased in Divisoria and arrive in a horse-drawn, two-wheeled *calesa* decked with bells. We have invited eighty children belonging to a variety of friends. That probably means that eighty ya-yas will come, too. We are excited.

Kristin floats around all the time in my old strapless yellow net formal dress that she found in the attic of Pilgrims Inn on our visit home. Eric is chasing his sisters with a fly-swatter, Trina shouting loudly in protest, "Air-Wick, Air-Wick."

Baguio, again after Christmas. Soft breezes hush through the pine-like agoho trees, making the fan palms undulate slowly back and forth and snapping the branches of the bougainvillea against the roof of the house where we are staying. Taal volcano is sending up whispers of danger, although there is no visible molten lava. Saigon is a mess.

In terms of Bud's project, by January of 1968, the two universities, Ateneo de Manila and de la Salle, had formally agreed to combine their management programs. The potential merger had absorbed many people's time and thought. Under Bud's leadership, the Harvard Advisory Group had drawn up a comprehensive plan for the creation of the new school. In early April, George Baker, Dean of the Harvard Business School, came to see how the project was progressing. He was impressed. The Institute formed from the recently-merged graduate management programs of Ateneo de Manila and De la Salle was called the Asian Institute of Management (AIM). It had already received incredible support from the business community in Manila in terms of donations for the land and the building. Nineteen faculty chairs had been generously endowed. President Marcos had provided money for a student loan program. The feasibility studies were complete, and the architect's plans for the new building had been drawn.

(AIM officially opened its doors a year later in 1969. It subsequently emerged as the first graduate school of management in Asia to offer a fully-accredited MBA program.)

Everyone wanted Bud to stay and help get AIM off to a good start, but we had begun to feel ready to return to the States. In my opinion, at least, we risked being pampered! I wanted our children to grow up with sturdy, understated Yankee values, those values that I had almost lost at the International Date Line. I wanted them to learn to do things for themselves in order to build character!

After the push to create AIM, Bud was scheduled to return to take up his faculty responsibilities at the Harvard Business School in the 1968 fall term. Before moving back to the States, however, Bud and I had the opportunity to take several trips both in the Philippines and elsewhere in Asia. I described these trips in letters to my family:

> We have just bought *The Golden Guide to Asia* and are actively planning a trip in late spring to Angkor Wat in Cambodia and to Rajasthan in northwest India. Before that, in April, we plan to travel to Bongabong, a mountainous

region on the island of Mindoro, to visit one of the eight indigenous tribes called Mangyans that live there. In fact, each of the tribes has its own language and customs. From what we understand, the tribe that we will visit has no distinctive rituals. Members of the tribe live in bamboo huts cantilevered over steep hillsides communicating from hut to hut with a bird-like song. They carve messages on bamboo cylinders in what looks somewhat like cuneiform writing. I learned that it is a syllabic Indic script.

Senor Madarang, the artist friend with whom we are going is the head of Philippine Women's University School of Fine Arts. He wants to trace some of this unique script to preserve it. He visits the tribe occasionally and represents its interests in Manila when needed. He told us to bring beads and matches and packages of soap powder. Apparently, ringworm is a real problem, so the artist will not see the chief or any tribal member until they have washed themselves with our packaged soap under a nearby waterfall. We will take malaria suppressant pills before we go and protection against leeches and mosquitos and jungle bugs.

Later:

Our trip to Mindoro and the Mangyans was challenging and fascinating. We left just before midnight from the public bus station in Manila. Sharing the bus with local families and baskets of chickens, we slept sitting upright on wooden seats. About four in the morning, we got off the bus, ate some bread and hard-boiled eggs at a fly-infested butcher shop and boarded a rusty, grimy local ferry packed with island people, pigs, chickens, and sugarcane. It was a rough crossing to the island of Mindoro. On land once again, we boarded another local bus and jostled on bumpy tracks for four hours. Then we started our five-hour trek on foot into the mountains.

En route, we came across an isolated barrio and joined the tiny population in a fiesta. Some of the men were dressed up as bushes, having clothed themselves in branches and leaves. One of them asked me to dance and off we went on the swept dirt to the music of a harmonica and a gasoline-can drum. I helped pound yucca roots to make into cakes.

We left the trail that bordered a river and followed a dry river bed through the jungle until at last we reached the nipa hut of the Mangyan chief. Wearing a loincloth, he greeted us with a broad betel nut-blackened smile. The tribe practices slash-and-burn farming, terrible for the environment. In order to create open land for their tiny plots, they clear the jungle growth with their bolos, then burn the area. Without plant roots to hold the soil, the land is quickly eroded. And we were encouraging this destruction by bringing them matches as gifts!

Following a slim, wiry tribal member who wore a loincloth and carried a monkey on his shoulder, we clambered up a steep slope to visit his tiny dark nipa hut cantilevered out over the steep slope, chickens and pigs rooting about underneath. We slept for a few nights in the chief's nipa hut with his family, drops of rain coming through the cogon grass roof and splattering onto the floor. I thought of the anthropologist Margaret Mead and wondered how she would have observed this group. Our artist friend was pleased with his rubbings of the syllabic script and will display them at some point in a gallery in Manila.

> Bud and I cut short the five-hour return hike to the bus by plunging fully-clothed into the fast-flowing river and floating downstream with the current toward our destination. No piranhas in Philippine rivers.

Upon our return to Manila, I opened a six-week summer play school in our house for twenty children, ages three and four, good companions for Trina and Eric. Kristin, meanwhile, was prospering in a summer-session repeat of the first grade. Now, she got everything right. Her previous experience in first grade had been pretty rough, given that she had had her tonsils out during the year and had been the youngest in her highly structured class. Kristin now rode home on the school bus and changed immediately into the old yellow net strapless evening dress. Trina loved her school, with all the singing and dancing. Trina caught a large, live frog at school one day and brought it home to keep. It escaped.

Once again in Baguio, I wrote to my parents:

> How we wish that you were here in Baguio with us. Clear, cool, pine-scented air, a wonderful change from Manila's steamy atmosphere. The sun shines in the morning. The rain pours down in the afternoon, but we have our fireplace in the little cottage and hot cocoa. We came ten days ago and will be here for about a month while Bud is teaching in an Advanced Management Program sponsored by HBS.
>
> At one point, we left Gloria in charge of Trina and Eric and drove with Kristin for eight hours up a tortuous route through the fog to the mountain municipality of Bontoc.

The next day, we followed a curving, curling road for another three hours until we reached the Ifugao province and the Eighth Wonder of the World, the Banaue Rice Terraces, carved by hand on the steep slopes about 2,000 years ago. Man will literally re-shape mountains to get rice.

The Ifugao (like the Illongots) were a head-hunting tribe, until head-hunting was banned in the 1930s. The tribal men we encountered wore G-strings. The women wove python bones through their shiny black hair to protect themselves, we learned, in childbirth and against lightning. We visited the circular, walled council rooms of the men where the men crouched and talked over tribal events, smoking cigars inside their pipes and drinking rice wine. Revenge statues stood beside the council house, the preserved human heads on the statues giving status to the council. The Ifugao sing an epic poem called the *Hudhud* dealing with their hero ancestors. They value kinship. Disputes are settled by wrestling. Until the practice of head-hunting was banned, the Ifugao collected, preserved and used the heads of their enemies in rituals, perhaps thinking that by doing so, they might absorb the enemy's life force.

A full moon. A spire-like tree where the gods live. Anyone who cuts it down will face instant death. Just-harvested rice bunched into dripping, heavy-beaded clusters lie on the ground just outside the huts. Pigs are everywhere, their grunting noises competing with the delicate sounds of the nose flutes, the deep tonal sounds of the gongs and the yipping of the barrio curs, scrawny and slinking. Pigs represent wealth and the ability to make sacrifices.

On the return trip, we waited for six hours while men used shovels to clear the mountain road from an immense landslide. Then we rocketed at top speed across the landslide area so that we wouldn't start another slide. And down again into the thick fog.

We were in the vicinity of the Benguet Gold Mine, so why not? We descended the next day 3,500 feet into its torrid depths. What men will do to find a thin vein of gold!"

By September, we were again back in Manila. There were extravagant parties, almost every night. People were charming and hospitable, but I had begun to tire of the opulence and the superficial conversations. The movers had come to pack things up for the sea shipment. They packed virtually everything. We had moved into the survival kit stage. The Ford Foundation provided the few things we needed to hold us over until our departure. A little apprehensive, I wrote home:

I love the thought of coming home to family and friends, but I truly dread the thought of shopping and cooking and washing dishes and car-pooling and the loneliness and isolation I will probably feel on rainy, snowy days while I vacuum and clean and do the laundry. Uh-oh. I guess I have been hopelessly spoiled during these past two years. I have begun to think of ways to get much needed help, including hiring someone and spending all of the money that we would have-spent if Gloria had come with us.

I have spent hours talking with the children, trying to prepare them for the fact that there won't be a Gloria, a Tina, or a Freddie back in America, but there will be snow and grandparents. I don't tell them that I want to take them home so that they will develop strong characters. I have a sneaking suspicion that it might be *my* character that will be tested and developed, as I will be the one who cares for the children, does the laundry, cooks, cleans, car-pools, shops, volunteers, etc., all the things that Kristin announced to our Filipino neighbor that American mothers do. At least, there won't be diapers! I am endlessly grateful to Gloria and Tina for all of their help during these last two demanding and important toddler years.

Eric just came in with Heather, his little girl friend from across the street. He is busy collecting hats for the trip back to the States—a sailor hat, a cat hat, a hat from Kashmir, a straw hat. He carries a big paper bag with him everywhere. When we clean it out, we find crayons, cookies and cockroaches. These artifacts will not go into his suitcase. Trina wishes that the turtle could come with us . . . and the cat. I have gently persuaded Kristin, now age six, to leave the yellow, strapless net gown behind. She has gone off to say good-by to her many friends in San Lorenzo Village. Whenever anyone mentions grandmothers or grandfathers, Eric proudly asserts, "I have one."

In September, Bud and I are planning a two-week trip to Cambodia, Thailand, India, Nepal, and Hong Kong. It may be our last chance to visit these places, so we are taking advantage of it.

The highlight of that trip was Kathmandu in Nepal. Kathmandu is a fascinating, almost medieval, city, its religion a synthesis of Buddhism and Hinduism with its gods, monkeys, and holy men. All against a stunning mountain background, the surrounding area alive with communities of Sherpas.

We stayed in the Royal Hotel. Sir Edmund Hillary, the first man to summit Mt. Everest, arrived the day we left. The hotel was a former palace and was quite dilapidated. Vast bedrooms, uncomfortable furniture, intermittent electricity, a tub that ran brassy-colored lukewarm water, awful food, but to us, a fabulous atmosphere.

Barry Bishop, a member of the American Expedition on Everest sponsored by National Geographic, was living in a trailer next to the hotel with his wife and two children, ages two and four. The family was on its way to spend a year or more in a relatively unexplored region on the Tibetan border in northwestern Nepal where he would work on his doctoral thesis. They had freeze-dried food, enough for two meals a week for the children for a year. Otherwise, they planned to live off the land. They would wear down pajamas day and night and read and play games in their tent. We drank beer with Barry in a dark corner of the gloomy, historic hotel, while he told us of losing toes from frostbite on one of his mountain ascents and how dedicated he was to the Sherpas.

We had been depressed by the poverty in the Philippines, but the poverty in India was staggering. People were living on the sidewalks in Calcutta along with rodents and flies. Beggars were everywhere pleading for baksheesh. There was an atmosphere of death. Death is more than an atmosphere in Varanasi. It is the essence of the city. People come there to die and to be cremated in this sacred city on the Ganges. It is believed that when a body is cremated there, the human soul is freed from the endless cycle of rebirth. I have heard that in certain castes, the eldest son has to crack the skull of the parent during the cremation ceremony, so that the dead parent's spirit can be released.

In Agra, the Taj Mahal literally did take my breath away. Seen from a distance, its elegance is awe-inspiring. Once inside, I was incredulous at the beauty and refinement of the inlay work, thousands of semi-precious stones set in marble. Stunning as they are, photographs of the Taj Mahal don't do it justice.

We visited Jodhpur, Jaipur, and Udaipur in Rajasthan in northwest India and drove for two days across the Thar Desert, the driest part of Rajasthan. Then, from Delhi, we flew to Bangkok and from there in a small plane to Angkor Wat in Cambodia. There were no hotels there, at that time, and no tourists. We stayed in a bunker used by French archaeologists who had come to excavate the stone temples, part of the Khmer Empire. The temples had been built by the Hindus in the early thirteenth century and dedicated to the Hindu god Vishnu.

Later, they were transformed into temples dedicated to Buddha. Buddhist priests in saffron robes and shaved heads were wandering about, chanting. Bats flew out of the temples that stank of their feces. Thick vines and the serpentine roots of ficus trees were strangling the temples, gripping and clawing at the stones. Over the centuries, the wooden lintels over temple entrances had been devoured by termites and moisture and had collapsed, weakening the rest of the temple structure. It was hot and muggy. We were well aware that the Vietnam War was being fought nearby, just over the border.

Returning to Manila, I wrote to my family:

> We find that the establishment of the Asian Institute of Management has created enormous excitement. Applications are open. Steve Fuller has agreed to take the job as dean for the first two or three years. He will be tremendous. Everyone wants Bud to stay. The Lopezes are planning something for

our last night here, October 18. I'm not sure, but I think that President Marcos and his wife, Imelda, will be there. It really is quite something to create a new school in two years, in a foreign country, and in a culture not known for philanthropy.

Last evening after a small farewell dinner, Father Donelan, the President of the Jesuit University, Ateneo de Manila, gave me a small, gold pendant as a parting gift. The next day, the Brothers at De La Salle College presented me with a wooden jewel box inlaid with mother-of-pearl. I will remember these wonderful friends.

Our stay in the Philippines has exceeded all of my expectations. We came seeking new adventures in, to us, an unknown part of the world. We have had them, mind-opening experiences, one streaming into another. We have learned so much, not only about life in the Philippines and certain corners of Asia, but about ourselves. The next chapter of our life at home in New England will be an adventure also, I'm certain, but of a different sort. I only hope that I will be up to the new challenges, whatever they may be.

Today, our house is empty, like a cave, no furniture, no pillows . . . just memories.

Fifty years later, on November 17, 2018, there were speeches honoring the founders of the Asian Institute of Management. Over 500 guests came to the Shangri-la Hotel in Makati to hear about the origins of AIM, its present activities, and its vision for the future. Bud has remained on the AIM Board of Governors during these past decades, but except for a visit to Baguio in 1969 and a visit on the twenty-fifth anniversary of AIM, this was my first trip back to the Philippines since the mid-1960s. On our visit twentyfive years ago, I had learned that the International Cooperative Pre-School had grown into an elementary school housed in a three-story building near AIM in Makati. I didn't ask about the school on this visit.

What was different after fifty years? Crowds of people everywhere. The population of the Philippines today is 105 million, more than three times its size in 1966. Skyscrapers. Bumper to bumper traffic. Trees and buildings had grown so tall in Makati surrounding the Asian Institute of Management that the building seemed smaller than I remembered. San Lorenzo Village seemed more congested, too, and darker because of the tall trees. There was no nipa hut in the front yard of 22 Tolentino, and I couldn't find the children's park at the end of the street where Eric had dazzled everyone with his athletic ability. In my mind's eye, though, I clearly saw Trina and Kristin coming down the street, mounted on the red papier-mâché horse drawn by Gloria.

Another difference was that Ferdinand Marcos, a progressive president who became a dictator, died in exile in Hawaii in 1989. He was accused of stealing ten billion dollars from the Philippines. On November 9, 2018, the Philippine court arrested his wife, Imelda, and sentenced her to forty-two years in prison on similar charges of theft and corruption. Duterte, the current, controversial President of the Philippines and an admirer of Marcos, is trying to resurrect Marcos's reputation.

Different, too, was the suspicion, as reported in the *Manila Times*, that the Chinese were taking over the Philippines as part of their world-wide Belt and Road Initiative. While we were there as guests in the Shangri-La Hotel, Xi Jinping, the Head of the Communist Party and the President of the People's Republic of China, was also in residence. He had come to offer a loan to the controversial Philippine President Duterte: "I will loan you money for this or that special project."

To himself, I imagine that President Xi was saying: *Of course, I know that you can never repay it. We Chinese are patient. Just give us the South China Sea, so that we can continue to create our islands and maybe eventually, you can cede to us the Philippines itself with all of your country's raw materials, mangoes, pineapples and fish.* On November 21, 2018, the editorial in the *Philippine Star News* read, "The government is gift-wrapping our sovereignty and territory in exchange for being the next debt colony of China. We are displaying a defeatist and meek attitude in the face of China's aggression."

What was the same? The heat, the humidity, and, yes, the poverty. More than that was the fact that everywhere and from everyone we received the same warm, relaxed, generous hospitality and the lovely radiant, heart-warming smiles that we remembered. I was glad to touch down once again in that special world full of so many smiles and brilliant memories.

Chapter Eight

Family Life

Belmont, Massachusetts, and Maine
(1968–1974)

America was in an uproar when we returned from the Philippines in late-October, 1968. And with good reason. Martin Luther King had been assassinated in April of that year. Bobby Kennedy had been shot and killed two months later. In Chicago, in August, just before our return, the Democratic National Convention had turned violent with students and activists protesting the war in Vietnam. I could sense the fear and anger in the air the moment we entered the airport in San Francisco. Although we had returned to the States briefly in 1963, my focus throughout the transforming decade of the 1960s had been on caring for our young family and its needs. I wasn't aware of how drastically U.S. culture had changed during the years that we had been living abroad. In Manila, we had read about some hostile student actions, such as Princeton students ejecting a dean from his office in April 1968 and leaving him face-down on the hallway floor. That story seemed outrageous and impossible to believe. But we had no idea how thoroughly this angry fever had permeated the country. America was on fire.

People seemed untethered from traditional behavioral norms. Perhaps during the decades of the 1940s and 1950s, adults had indeed lived conventional, restricted, and predictable lives, but the extent of this cultural revolution was stunning. Young people seemed to have lost respect for all authority figures, including parents and teachers and certainly the government leaders who had sent them to Vietnam and who continued to deny black citizens their civil rights. The youth openly and loudly criticized and insulted people in power. Although I agreed with many of their criticisms, I was distressed and alarmed. Was the hostility and violence going to bring about change?

My mind kept turning back to the way the Filipino children were taught to respect their elders. A child entering a room with a seated elder would honor the elder by taking his hand and kissing the back of it. A child would never talk back to an adult or interrupt an adult conversation. This behavior contrasted sharply with what I was observing in American households at the time with children talking back freely to their parents and in other ways showing no respect. Clearly, we had been living in another world and had missed much of a decade, the ten years that were becoming known as The Sixties. I had so much to learn.

The revolution even touched my parents. My brother George left the University of Colorado in his last semester and drove to Alaska to homestead. My brother Franklin, four years younger than George, left his studies at St. Lawrence University in New York state. At some point, he was arrested for having a small amount of marijuana in his car, an incident that stayed on his record for years, until the family hired a lawyer to have it expunged.

During this tumultuous time, my younger sister Anne protested vehemently about the hypocrisy of our leaders in the areas of civil rights, women's rights, and the environment.

Maple trees in New England had burst into full glorious color when we moved into our rented three-story house at 75 Hillside Terrace in Belmont, Massachusetts a residential town near Cambridge. It was on a dead end street with a public elementary school within walking distance. We rented it for $350 a month. It was a perfect home during that first winter when Bud started teaching again at HBS.

I remember Kristin's first day at her new school, Payson Park. She walked into her classroom, met her teacher and was assigned a desk. She immediately cleaned it out and scrubbed it vigorously with damp paper towels. Then she stood at the classroom door and warmly greeted everyone who walked in.

Trina was not happy at the Ecole Bilingue. When she wanted to go to the bathroom, she had to ask permission in French. She thought the teachers should be more helpful and speak English.

I remember taking Eric to a neighborhood preschool that he didn't like, bribing him daily with a stop at the donut shop. I think he really missed Gloria. I felt the same way, especially when, during that first winter, all three children, ages six, four and three, came down with chickenpox. As anticipated, I was doing the nursing as well as all of the shopping, cooking, cleaning, laundry and carpooling. Kristin even remembers watching me iron sheets and pillowcases in the basement. I can't believe that I considered ironing sheets to be a priority.

During a raging blizzard in February 1969, Trina was determined to get out in the snow and build a fort. The fort had five rooms, including a kitchen, with connecting passageways and tunnels. I remember Trina swaggering about in her new blue jeans, slung low. Her nickname then was Pistol. In her excitement at building the fort, she stepped out of one of her red boots which did not surface until spring.

I recently came across some notes that I made for myself when we had just returned from the Philippines. I obviously felt that I had the major responsibility for raising three young children, and I was clearly concerned about their upbringing. Quickly, on the back of a brown paper grocery bag, I jotted down a list for myself of matters that I thought were important guidelines for the children. Among them were:

- You should always stand up for what is right.
- You should not, without thinking, follow a leader. In fact, you should try to be the leader, a good and kind one.
- You should always tell the truth, without exception.
- You should not tell jokes which are cruel and unkind. Your friends might laugh for a moment, but they will quickly lose respect for you.
- You should be polite at the table and try to have beautiful table manners.
- You should always try to help others and to show respect toward your parents, teachers, older people and especially toward people who seem different.

Critical to my child-rearing efforts was my strong belief during these early years that the children should grow up without television's seductive messages. When we finally purchased a small, second-hand TV with a broken on/off knob, I would hide it in the shower or the laundry basket when Bud and I went out for dinner. On some occasions, we would put the portable TV in the back of the car and take it with us. The channels could only be changed by using a dinner fork.

On April 9, 1969, dozens of students protesting the Vietnam War broke into Harvard University's main administrative building, evicted a number of deans and opened University files. President Pusey called in the state police who arrived at dawn in riot gear. The students were outraged and went on strike. Thousands of demonstrators filled the stands in the Harvard Stadium. I was there and can testify to the anger of the huge crowd, the shouting, the jeering and cheering, the protest banners held high.

It must have been about this time that Bud came home one afternoon, pale and shaken. He had been in the middle of giving an exam at HBS when there was a bomb threat in the building. The building was evacuated, and the students dismissed, sent home to complete the exam on the honor system. No grades were given. This was just another example of the student protests, riots, and anti-Vietnam war and civil rights demonstrations that were shaking academic institutions across the country.

Sometime in the late summer of 1969, we purchased a house at 15 Pinehurst Road, also in Belmont. It was located on a dead-end street off of Concord Avenue on Belmont Hill between Day School Lane and Old Concord Road, a dirt road that had once been a stagecoach route. We loved living there under the thirty-foot pine tree by the front door. The neighborhood was full of charming, interesting, and fun-loving families who were dedicated to providing wholesome homes for their children. Our children ran in and out of the houses of these families. The friends we made—the Webbs, the Hastings, the Brosios, the Perkins, and the Barss, Laskaris, and the Harris families—have lasted a lifetime. We often shared Thanksgivings and other important occasions with the Gunness family who lived nearby.

Those were wonderful years for Bud and for me as we continued creating a home and a life. We could walk down Old Concord Road to the public library and to the Winn Brook School, the public elementary school that our children attended. We could walk to the Unitarian Church, too, although I felt that it was important to expose the children to other forms of worship as well. I remember taking them to a Jewish temple, a Greek Orthodox church, and a Quaker meeting. We skated on the little pond in the woods across Concord Avenue and went sledding behind our house down a hill that overlooked Boston. We went caroling with lanterns in the neighborhood at Christmas and delivered May baskets to our neighbors in the spring. We played neighborhood soccer on the adjacent field belonging to the Belmont Day School. We hosted a square dance in our basement where the neighborhood children also rehearsed *The Wind in the Willows* for a later performance at the Day School. Kristin was Mole and Trina and Eric were in charge of acting out the part of the wind, waving willow branches over the stage set. Eric learned to ski on the gentle slope of our back yard where all three children created a ski resort complete with a detailed trail map drawn by Kristin. Eric occasionally slept in his sleeping bag in the garage with his beloved rabbit. Sometimes, in our eagerness to create a memorable childhood, we created a disaster. One spring, Bud and I hid Easter eggs in the woods near the pond, not realizing until Trina began screaming in anguish that we had concealed the eggs in thickets of poison ivy! We put poor suffering Trina in a tub of cool water, then gently covered her blistering, itching skin with calamine lotion.

The children did well at the Winn Brook School. Kristin played the role of Buttercup, peddling treacle and toffee in *H.M.S. Pinafore* in the school play. Trina was master of the playground at recess, swinging high on the swing set and moving fast across the monkey bars. Both Trina and Eric won presidential fitness awards for their running speed, jumping distance and number of sit-ups and chin-ups. They both remember climbing the towering pine tree in front of the house. To earn pocket money, the children set up a lemonade stand in the street at the end of our driveway.

We began spending a month or so during the summers on Isle au Haut, an island with a working lighthouse in the Penobscot Bay off the Maine coast, reached by the mail boat from Stonington, Maine. Bordered here and there with balsam trees, sweet fern, and a plant called pearly-everlasting, a single mostly dirt road circled the island. Paths through the pine woods were emerald green with ferns and velvety moss. A few years earlier, my seafaring Uncle Lloyd, my mother's younger brother, had purchased the island's original farmhouse on Moores Harbor where we stayed several times. In later years, from Anne Davidson, we rented the original icehouse on the hill above the farmhouse with its cistern to catch rainwater, its pump above the kitchen sink, and its outhouse. Two lively and generous families, the Jacobuses and the Sawyers, shared the harbor.

Uncle Lloyd had an interesting career. After attending MIT where he studied naval architecture and marine engineering, he worked with Admiral Hyman Rickover to help develop the first nuclear-powered submarine. After the end of World War II, he went on to run four major United States shipyards. Later, after learning about the dangers of nuclear power, he regretted his work on nuclear submarines and began to design container ships that could be run partly on wind power. He started a company called Windships.

Uncle Lloyd was well-known for winning sailing races sponsored by yacht clubs along the East Coast. In 1978, in his mid-sixties, he sailed alone to Norway in his wooden Herreshoff-designed racing boat, the *Cockatoo II*, a class of boat known as a New York 30. After sailing up the west coast of Norway, Uncle Lloyd left the boat in the Lofoten Islands over the winter. The following summer, with his son, Henry, he set sail for New England, wanting to replicate the voyage of his grandfather, Ole Bergeson, who had sailed from Norway across the Atlantic in 1857. The *Cockatoo II* sprang a leak however, and in spite of assistance from the crew of a nearby container ship, it sank in heavy seas 600 miles south of Iceland. I have always admired Uncle Lloyd's independent spirit and his daring. His voyage is fully described in several issues of *Cruising World*. ("A Death in the Family: The Loss of Cockatoo II," Lloyd Bergeson, *Cruising World*, 1/10/80)

On clear days on Isle au Haut, the view from the top of Duck Mountain over the island and the sea was stunning, the brilliant blue sea speckled with white sails. We could bathe in the cool, clear water of the creek that flowed through the woods and emptied into the harbor. Sometimes, we would pile into the back of a worn-out pick-up truck and drive through the tiny village to Long Pond for a swim or to Boom Beach to lie on the smooth rocks and watch plumes of spray kicked up by thunderous waves. We would stop at the island's only store on the way home to pick up some island gossip along with a Popsicle or an ice cream sandwich. We learned of weddings that had been held and new babies born on the island.

And we learned of horrific island tragedies. Four teenage island boys, fishermen's sons, died when their boat capsized near the island on a stormy night. The daughter of a beloved island minister set fire to herself in a suicide attempt. The island community was tiny. Everyone shared joys and sorrows.

In addition to the store, the island had a one-room schoolhouse, where the school teacher educated island children in grades one through eight. There was also a town hall, a handsome granite building, that housed both the library as well as a spacious room for community gatherings, theater productions and dancing the polka. The slender white steeple of the church was often the first glimpse of the island from the mail boat. I wish I could remember the name of the sparrow whose liquid song made me pause on my walks in the late afternoons and catch my breath.

The role of wife, homemaker, and mother during this period in my life was deeply fulfilling. I knew that I was needed by each member of my family. My family was my focus. I gave it all of the imagination, intelligence, and organizational skill that I possessed. Nevertheless, once the fall came and the children had gone back to school, I craved more involvement with the community. During the six years, between 1968 when we returned from the Philippines and 1974 when Bud became President of Babson College and we moved to Wellesley, I threw myself into volunteer activities.

"When I get out of here, I am going to find my wife and kill her!" The Metropolitan State Mental Hospital was not far from our house. I worked there for a year or so as a Case Aid volunteer. My assignment was to build trust with Frank who had previously been incarcerated in the Bridgewater State Prison for the Criminally Insane. After our relationship was established and he trusted me, I was to ask him what he planned to do should he be released from Met State. He gave the above answer which I passed on to the director as I had been instructed. Frank was furious. He had been punished by being "put in pajamas" and placed in the locked ward. He claimed that he would kill me, if he saw me again. I called the office, asking what I should do. "Come in," I was told, "meet with him." A young man, a Conscientious Objector who was working at the hospital in place of serving in Vietnam, met me and opened the door to a small room. "I will let Frank in."

I was alone in the room and frightened, particularly since Frank knew where I lived. Frank came in, glaring at me, his face contorted in anger, his fists in tight balls. "You got me punished," he shouted. "I thought I could trust you." There was not much I could say. "I'm sorry, Frank," I said in a soft voice. His reaction was amazing. Maybe no one had ever apologized to him. His fists unclenched. He slumped. "Okay," he said, looking at the floor. "I'm sorry." Powerful words. A lesson, I thought, in how to deflect anger.

For the Belmont League of Women Voters, I helped organize a two-year study of the guidance and student personnel service of the Belmont public school system, as well as serving as co-chairman (we weren't called *chairs* at that time) of the Belmont Committee on Open Education and as co-chairman with Bud of the Winn Brook PTA. I asked for Bud's help because I didn't feel confident enough at the time to handle that position myself.

Wanting to feel tied once again to the international community and to the world of adventure, I volunteered as Director of Museum Services for Earthwatch, a nonprofit organization located in Belmont that continues to this day to match scholars and scientists with lay volunteers in scientific field research projects around the world.

For a year, I volunteered at MIT as an advisor to the wives of "foreign" students, as they were called then. Their husbands, graduate students from around the world, were working during the day in their labs, leaving their wives alone in their apartments, terrified to step outside into what they had heard were our violent American streets. As advisors, we attended a number of lectures, so that we could better understand the customs of countries, like Egypt and the Sudan, from which some of these women had come. I remember one lecture in particular on female genital circumcision. I was shocked by the cruelty of the operation.

In mid-July 1969, I flew back across the Pacific to the Philippines, traveling alone this time with Trina and Eric while Kristin visited her Sorenson grandparents in Mansfield, Ohio. Bud, already in Baguio, was again teaching the advanced management class. The trip seemed endless, with stops in Hawaii and Guam, but it was heaven to be back in Baguio, so beautiful and peaceful. On July 20, 1969, the *Eagle*, the Apollo 11 spacecraft, landed on the moon. I described the landing in a letter to my parents:

> It's unbelievable! Do you remember when we used to look up at the night sky and imagine seeing The Man in the Moon? Now a man has landed on the moon! "One small step for man; one giant leap for mankind." Those were the words spoken by mission commander Neil Armstrong and heard around the world. There was unbelievable suspense waiting until the *Eagle* had landed, watching the tendril-like leg swaying tentatively trying to make contact with the surface of the moon. There was the overwhelming

> admiration for the technical sophistication and the astronauts' rigorous, disciplined training that allowed this accomplishment. But there was also the apprehension that something had to go wrong and the amazement when the take-off from the moon went well, too. To say nothing of the romance of capturing solar wind! We thought of you as we sat in the fire station of the military airbase here in Baguio, listening to the voices of Neil Armstrong and Buzz Aldrin as the LEM was guided to a touch-down spot and as it took off again. They are not yet safely back on Earth, but I expect they will make it. I hope that you saw it all. It makes the exploration of Mars seem possible. That will really be something.

Man's landing on the moon as well as the photograph called *Earthrise* taken six months earlier on Christmas Eve, December 24, 1968 by the astronaut Bill Anders, are credited with having made the world aware of the beauty as well as the fragility of our planet Earth. The photograph *Earthrise* shows our incandescent blue planet rising above the rough grimy surface of the moon. It affected me deeply, increasing my appreciation of our planet's special place in the vast, dark, icy cosmos. The photograph became to some extent the emblem of the nascent environmental movement. I can still see it in my mind's eye.

American culture was still in a period of tumultuous transition when we returned from Baguio that summer. In mid-August 1969, 400,000 young people gathered in Woodstock, New York to attend a rock concert. The massive gathering revealed a new generation's independence from authority figures and social and cultural conventions. The images of the bacchanalian revelers smoking marijuana and celebrating peace, music, and free love were striking and caught the attention of the world.

April 22, 1970 was the first Earth Day. The words *environmentalism* and *ecology* were introduced. I was alarmed and frightened when I read Rachel Carson's book *Silent Spring*. I learned that we were destroying our beautiful planet and that the rate of destruction seemed to be out of control. Rachel Carson encouraged us to think of ourselves as stewards of the planet, but it was clear that in 1970 we hadn't fully appreciated the extent to which we citizens had to be involved. Our planet was in jeopardy. Trash, especially plastic trash, was clogging our rivers and oceans. Chemicals sprayed on our plants as weed-killers and insecticides were killing the soil and poisoning our aquifers. The smoke from burning coal and fossil fuels was fouling the air and increasing the rate of climate change.

On that first Earth Day, we were just becoming aware of how terribly Gaia, our Mother Earth, was suffering. This was a new reality for me. I was both heart-broken by what I was learning and unsure that government leaders would step forward to address the situation. I wondered whether it was going to be the role of women, not only to nurture and protect their children and families, but to nurture and protect the planet itself. Was saving Mother Earth going to be a woman's issue and responsibility?

On May 4, 1970, members of the Ohio National Guard killed four unarmed college students at Kent State University in Ohio. The students were protesting the pre-emptive bombing of Cambodia which President Nixon and Secretary of State Kissinger had authorized. On May 9, 1970, 100,000 protesters gathered in front of the White House. Clearly, we had returned to a country in crisis.

During these turbulent and complicated years, it was wonderful to be able to drive to Stockbridge during weekends and holidays and to spend time in the familiar, supportive, and creative environment of Pilgrims Inn. No longer did a drive from Boston involve twisting and turning to climb over Jacob's Ladder as it had in my childhood. We sped now for 140 miles along a parallel road, the Massachusetts Turnpike.

Bud and I continued to travel, combining his work with pleasure. In the summer of 1971, we left Trina and Eric with Grandma and Grandpa Sorenson in Ohio and took Kristin with us on a European study tour. We bicycled on Belle-Isle off the north-western coast of France and studied French history in the castles of the Loire Valley. We slept under fluffy duvets in a hotel on the shores of Lake Geneva in Pully. Under the stern watch of border guards in their towers who did not return our waves and smiles, we passed through Checkpoint Charlie in the Berlin Wall, the emblem of the Cold War between Russia and the United States. We found East Berlin to be almost deserted, depressing and scary. In Scotland, we confirmed the existence of the Loch Ness monster. We arrived finally in Cambridge, England, where Bud was teaching a summer management course at Emmanuel College. In that beautiful town, we punted on the River Cam and made brass rubbings in local churches of Sir Roger Trumpington and other medieval knights. "Eight times seven is fifty-six!" Kristin and I worked hard that summer on multiplication tables.

In 1973, I began to study for a Master's Degree in Education at Lesley College in Cambridge. The following year, I received both my degree and Massachusetts Certification as an elementary-school teacher with an emphasis on teaching children with specific learning disabilities. When the results were in, I found that I was in the top five percent of those taking the National Teacher's Examination. I was struck on the day of the examination that only women were taking the teachers' exam. There was a separate exam that day for school principals. Only men, I noticed, took the principals' exam.

Chapter Nine

Babson College

and the White Paper (1974–1981)

In 1974, the same year that Richard Nixon resigned in disgrace from the presidency, Bud accepted the offer to become the seventh President of Babson College in Wellesley. Bud was forty-one years old. I was thirty-five and our children were twelve, ten, and nine. We moved into the President's Residence at 56 Whiting Road, a house with eight bedrooms and a spacious yard. We lived there for seven exciting, enriching and challenging years.

Bud gave an inspiring Inaugural Address, painting a picture of the great things Babson College could achieve. I was in full support of his vision for the college and helped in every way that I could, including entertaining the many college constituencies. We had catering help for important college events and a housekeeper who came once a week. Even though the college gave us some money to make improvements to the President's Residence, Bud and I preferred to direct that money to student scholarships, faculty salaries, or to the library. Babson College at that time did not have an endowment or even an alumni association. Sometimes, our children shared in Bud's efforts to fundraise: "I knew I made a difference," said Eric proudly, when he learned of the gift to the college of four million dollars from Olin Foundation. Eric took some credit because he often helped out at college functions in our home.

Being hospitable was not always easy, however. "You cannot entertain them! You must cancel your invitation!" A Russian history professor at Wellesley called me on the phone one day. "You haven't heard? The Russians have just invaded Afghanistan!" In 1980, preparing for the Lake Placid Olympics, the Russian Olympic figure skating team had made arrangements to practice for a few weeks on the newly-constructed ice skating rink at Babson We had agreed to host a late-afternoon reception.

Notwithstanding the professor's demand, we went ahead with our gathering, greeting the Olympic team when they arrived at our front door, wearing fur hats and heavy gray woolen coats. Their olive-drab uniforms were embroidered with a red hammer and sickle. Several "minders" were in attendance, and it was obvious from their appearance and their manner that they were officials from the KGB. There were no defections.

I showed our guests where to leave their coats. Then, to my astonishment, one of the female members of the team announced: "We go look now." Team members fanned out in all directions, opening closet and cabinet doors and pulling out drawers. They thoroughly explored the first and second floor but, fortunately, not the attic. This was lucky, because Trina and Eric had created a secret hiding place in a dark corner where they could hide one of the skaters, in case he or she decided to defect during the reception. Two of the Russian skaters went on to win gold medals at the Olympics.

Sometime shortly after 1976 when the Cultural Revolution ended in China, a young Chinese woman arrived at 56 Whiting Road. Her aunt, a professor at Wellesley College, knowing that we often invited international students to stay with us, had asked if her niece could live with us for the semester.

I will never forget the afternoon that our Chinese guest arrived. She laid out her few possessions in the comfortable bedroom on the third floor, then came down to the kitchen where I was preparing supper for our family. Our dog was curled up on a pad in the corner of the kitchen. "In China, we eat dogs!" she stated coldly. Then, a little later, "In China, we could fit thirty families into this house!"

Ours was an unfortunate match, made more so by the fact that thieves broke into our house shortly after her arrival and stole everything of even slight value that she had brought with her. I replaced her possessions as best I could, then drove her into Cambridge where she had found lodging with other Chinese families in a dark, crowded, noisy boarding house. She seemed happier there. I understood.

A family retainer, a *go-between*, arrived one morning from Japan. The Toyoda family had sent a fine gentleman to spend time in our house observing our family. The go-between was to determine whether to recommend our home to the Toyodas as an appropriate place for their son, Akio, to live for six months while he began his studies at Babson. The go-between must have given a good report, as Akio arrived one day with his suitcase and a big smile. He was a wonderful guest, thoughtful, polite, flexible, appreciative, and witty. Everyone in our family came to love him. Several years later, when Bud and I attended his wedding in Tokyo, he introduced us as "my American family." Knowing something about the refinements of the Japanese cuisine, I'm certain that

Akio struggled when he lived with us not only with my cooking but with its presentation. Eventually Akio followed in the footsteps of his father and grandfather, becoming the CEO of the Toyota Motor Company, a position he holds today.

It was challenging to keep up with all of the visitors. A Babson trustee laughingly reminded me for years following his term that he had spent one night in our guest room sleeping directly on the mattress pad, using the bedspread as a cover. I had forgotten to make the bed.

As the years passed, I was deeply proud of Bud and of the way that he was bringing life and a sense of pride to the college. I appreciated that it was important work. On the Babson campus, I could see that Bud was admired and treated with great respect. I was happy to see him shine at the endless campus and social events. He was sought after and had a voice that grew increasingly confident, "Hi, I'm Bud."

As time went on, however, while he was the star at these events, I began to feel more and more like a voiceless shadow. For example, how was I to answer the dreaded party question that always followed an introduction, "And what do you *do*?" I was tongue-tied. Responding that I was a loving wife and mother, a dedicated homemaker, and a willing and active volunteer, seemed to be a conversation stopper. Instead, I would murmur, "I'm Bud's wife." What I had been doing apparently was not interesting and, as I interpreted the flat response, not valued. I certainly did not want to enumerate my current life's obligations and complexity. I knew that I was making a difference in the lives of our children and in the life of the college. "But, what do you *do*?" Those asking the question seemed to be insisting that I give them a different answer.

Much later, I discovered that a better introductory question might be simply, "What interests you or makes you happy these days?"

How I would have liked to respond to the question as a professional somebody, someone whose life had societal value, "I am a lawyer, a doctor, an anthropologist, a botanist, a musician, a social worker." How validating to be able to give people my business card and to be paid a salary. I had graduated from Wellesley with a degree in Art History and with the strong message from the college and the culture of the time that my anticipated life course as a wife and mother was an honorable and worthy one.

What had happened? Why was my confidence so shaken? Why was I having an identity crisis? In the late 1970s, I was becoming aware that some of the wives in my suburban Wellesley neighborhood, having divorced their husbands, were stepping out on their own. The introduction of the Pill in 1960 had begun to free women from the feeling that child-bearing and child-rearing were an inevitable part of their lives. Also, divorce was easier to get and was no longer stigmatized. The first No-Fault Divorce Law had been passed in California in 1969 and similar laws were being passed across the country. Gone were the days when people at parties would point to a single woman and whisper behind their hands . . . "she's divorced."

One of my neighbors, a bright, attractive woman in her early thirties, told me in blunt terms, "I'm sick of being a wife and mother. I'm divorcing my husband and going back to school." Another neighborhood friend was spending all of her weekends at EST (Erhard Seminars Training, founded in 1971 by Werner Erhard) in which she was challenged to take responsibility for her own life. It was rumored that, because the group's facilitators depended on sensory deprivation and harsh verbal confrontation to change behavior, EST was a cult.

I began to see young women in my neighborhood leaving their houses in the mornings dressed in pinstriped suits and feminized ties. They told me when we met on the street that they were no longer looking for "jobs" as a secretaries, teachers or nurses. They were on "career paths." They said that they insisted at work on being called "women," not "girls." And they didn't fix or deliver the coffee.

Other women of my age were joining consciousness-raising groups in which they discussed the injustice of being fired from work for being pregnant. They told me that they were shocked to learn that flight attendants had to be a size four and that they were forbidden to marry. They told me that it was difficult for a woman to get credit in her own name. With these friends, I took a few classes on how to invest and how to manage money.

I also attended a class on how to be assertive, but not aggressive, as opposed to being subservient, submissive and accommodating. I bought and read the newly-published book *Our Bodies, Ourselves*, so that I could try to understand the things my mother had never told me about female sexuality. I was encouraged to learn that there was an effort in the legal world to treat rape and domestic abuse as crimes rather than the inalienable rights of men. I never read, but other women friends loved, Erica Jong's *Fear of Flying* and the new and popular feminist magazines like *Ms.* or *Cosmopolitan.*

As I understood it at the time, Betty Friedan in *The Feminine Mystique*, published in 1963, essentially derided the housewife, the poor soul who was both captive and slave in her home, spending her days praising her refrigerator and extolling the virtues of her washer, dryer, vacuum cleaner, and extraordinary furniture polish. In challenging the magazine, TV and radio ads that featured such images, Friedan inspired a revolution. She reserved special contempt for the educated housewife, the woman who had been to college then married but did not pursue paid work outside of the house. Some quotes:

> *"We can no longer ignore that voice within women that says: 'I want something more than my husband and my children and my home.'"*
>
> *"It is frightening when a woman finally realizes that there is no answer to the question 'Who am I?' except the voice inside herself."*
>
> *"Who knows what women can be when they are finally free to be themselves? Who knows what women's intelligence will contribute when it can be nourished without denying love?"*

I felt disoriented, caught in a powerful cultural shift. Affected by the creeping realization that I, an educated woman, was just a housewife, I began to feel that I was a just a housewife squared. Of course, I did not pose in high heels in front of my refrigerator, nor did I sing the praises of my floor polish. But I did shop, cook and clean, do the family laundry and carpool our children to schools and games while at the same time overseeing the President's Residence and grounds and supporting Babson College in a volunteer capacity in myriad ways. Clearly, I was not just a normal housewife. In Betty Friedan's eyes and in the eyes of the emerging women's liberation movement, I was a Super Housewife and therefore, I thought at the time, worthy of contempt. My confidence was deeply shaken. I felt that I had fallen into a trap. Having excelled and taken pride in playing by the rules of the traditional culture, I was now caught in limbo as the rules were changing dramatically for women of my generation.

I knew that raising a family, supporting Bud, fulfilling Babson's expectations as its First Lady, and volunteering for numerous nonprofits had value. The culture in which I had grown up had fully supported that path. As a group, women like me and most of my Wellesley classmates had been honored through the years for serving as the key to a smoothly-running and healthy society. Ironically, the new women's liberation movement did not liberate those of us who had excelled in the traditional way. Because the rules had radically changed mid-game, we found ourselves caught in a tangle of judgements concerning our roles that left us confused and questioning.

I didn't talk to anyone about my feelings, but one long weekend, while Bud was attending a board meeting in Europe, I crashed, although I could not clearly articulate why. All I knew was that I needed to get away, not only from Babson with its implicit expectations and obligations, but also from the children and from Bud. Bud was fulfilled by his position as president of the college, and I was happy for that. He had earned the kudos. He deserved them. But deep down, I had begun to feel empty, trapped in an invisible caretaking role. I found someone to take care of the children for a few nights and, without leaving a note with my whereabouts, took refuge in a hotel in Boston. I tried to reach a psychiatrist during that time, but no one was available. Talking to a professional at that moment probably would have been helpful.

When Bud returned, he tried to find me but was unsuccessful and began to worry. I called him when I was ready to talk. I shared my deep appreciation and gratitude for all that he had brought into my life: the excitement, the exposure to the world, the interesting friends, the financial support, the emotional support, the love and commitment. However, I told him, I felt that something was missing in my life. "I love you, Bud," I said, "and I'm truly proud of the job you are doing for the college. But as for me, I feel trivialized and pushed to my limit." I reminded him that, in addition to meeting the needs of our three active and growing children, I was overseeing the maintenance of the President's Residence and grounds and entertaining about 2,000 college guests a year in the college residence which was also our family home. "Please think of me from now on as your partner," I pleaded. "I am more than just a wife or a housewife, a word, by the way, that I deplore." Bud listened quietly and seemed to understand.

Now that I think back on that episode, I believe that what I was really trying to tell Bud was that I was exhausted. I couldn't keep playing the role and doing the job of being "the-wife-of." I was tired of being a "two-for." I was tired of standing alone at the front door to greet our guests, then finding myself hours later at the end of an event still standing alone at the front door. "Thank you so much for coming." I had had enough. In fact, in the late spring of our seventh and final year at Babson, if I saw someone coming up the front walk, I often fled through the kitchen and out the back door. I obviously needed to take the time to listen to "the voice inside myself," as Friedan recommended.

I continued believing in Bud and his vision for the college. But to demonstrate that I could function in the real world, I took a part-time job. For two years, I drove into Cambridge to tutor children with learning disabilities at the Shady Hill School. I also continued to volunteer at Wellesley College as a member of the Alumnae Board. Trying to build my self-confidence as an independent professional, I took a course in public speaking. At that point, though, I really wasn't sure that I had anything to say

Nearing the end of our seven-year tenure at Babson, I finally recovered my voice and the assurance that what I had been doing had merit. When the Presidential Search Committee set up a meeting with Bud to consider his replacement, I asked if I could speak with the committee as well. When we met on November 1, 1980, I presented the members of the committee with the following *White Paper* that I had written that describing both the role and the job of a college president's spouse.

To the Members of the Babson College Presidential Search Committee:

Thank you for inviting me to your meeting. I am grateful for the opportunity to share with you my views on what is involved in being the wife of a college president.

I would like to begin by saying that the last seven years have been for me marvelous and happy ones.

We became involved with Babson College at a time when my first priority was our family of three children whose ages when we arrived at Babson were eleven, nine, and eight. I considered our Babson activities to be a natural extension of our family activities, an enhancement in fact, of our family activities. Fortunately, everyone entered into this spirit and Babson College and our growing family seemed to mesh nicely.

My intention this morning is to describe to you both the ROLE that I have played and the JOB that I have done for Babson College.

I will also describe for you how other spouses are handling their positions at other academic institutions.

(In these remarks, *spouse* means *wife*, as college presidents have traditionally been men.)

And I will offer some suggestions to you as members of the search committee so that the spouse of the president whom you select will be aware of what is involved in this new position and will look upon it as an opportunity.

THE ROLE

The traditional college president's spouse has tended to adopt an attitude, assume a posture. You will recognize her.

- She is gracious, hospitable, tactful, discreet, and pleasant;
- She is quietly but totally supportive of her husband and of the institution that he has chosen to represent;
- She takes pains to learn about the college, keeps up on the day-to-day events, and tries to learn everyone's name and position. Somehow, however, she remains detached. She is well-informed, but diplomatically does not get involved in college matters. She does not embarrass the president.
- She accepts the responsibility of being a public person. She works hard at protecting her privacy and that of her family, if there are children involved.
- She makes herself available for college functions. She doesn't seem to mind that she does not have extended periods of time that she can call her own.
- She listens well, especially as her husband's confidant;
- She keeps her sense of humor and her perspective;
- She is aware.
- These qualities comprise what I call the ROLE. This is the image that comes to the minds of most people

when they think of a college president's wife. The ROLE is an attitude that the wife assumes. But it does not answer the question: But what does she do?

THE JOB

I would like to suggest today that, in addition to playing what sounds like a rather passive ROLE, the college president's wife is often expected to take on a substantial JOB. It is a job that requires physical energy and quantities of time. It requires organizational, administrative, and public relations skills in abundance. It requires commitment.

As it is not understood, this JOB is seldom outlined by search committees or college trustees. It is probably seldom understood or discussed in advance by the presidential candidates and their wives.

The JOB that I am about to describe is unavoidable. Especially, if the president and his wife are encouraged to live on campus in a college-owned house, the expectations are there.

This JOB has to be done, whether by a bewildered wife who is overwhelmed, by an informed spouse who finds that this is just her thing, or by a professional housekeeper cum executive secretary cum hostess (to be supervised, of course, by the spouse,) if, of course, she is lucky enough to find such a package.

For me, for the past seven years, this JOB has meant:

- being willing to take on the responsibility of being the caretaker of college property, the President's House and grounds. This has meant dealing almost daily with the college's buildings and grounds staff and knowing what is necessary and how things should be done;

- being willing to take on the responsibility of being the chief caterer. Not much cooking is involved, but there is much planning, preparation and working with and supervising the kitchen staff sent from the college as well as the occasional outside caterer;
- being willing to take on the responsibility of being chief housekeeper, supervising the help that comes to clean, making sure that house is always ready for guests, expected and unexpected;
- planning, preparing for and supervising over twenty scheduled events in the President's House during the school year;
- preparing for quickly and supervising about fifteen college-related but unscheduled events in the President's House during the school year.

During the past seven years, we have entertained over 14,000 guests in the President's House, the house that is also our home and the home of our three growing children who, of course, have their own very definite demands and needs. Students, parents of students, faculty members, members of the staff and the administration, trustees, alumni, members of the community and other neighboring academic institutions, and sometimes the spouses and families of these groups . . . all have been made welcome.

This JOB has also meant:

- attending, as a representative of the college, about twenty-five scheduled events a year on the campus, including appearances at trustee meetings, dedications and such;

- attending, as a representative of the college, about thirty unscheduled but college-related functions a year both on and off the campus including athletic events, dinners with students' parents, dinners with VIPs, visiting firemen, administrators from neighboring colleges, etc. (I have purposely separated the scheduled and unscheduled events to imply the state of readiness that has to exist.)
- being available and active on behalf of the college almost every weekend from the beginning of September to mid-October, for several weekends during the holiday season and during the weekends in late April and May.
- being on-call and active for entire weekends: Parents' Weekend, Winter Weekend, Homecoming Weekend and Commencement;
- traveling to meet alumni. I haven't done as much of this as there was to be done, but it could have been a substantial part of the JOB;
- attending seminars in which my husband was often a participant, partly out of interest, but often because I needed a chance to be with him, away from the college;
- keeping careful records of the way that I spent college money;
- making the extra phone call, writing thank-you notes, sending or arranging flowers, etc.
- keeping not only the college house and grounds, but also myself and the children ready at all times, so that we would all reflect positively on the college.

This is the JOB that is there. This is the JOB that is unavoidable. Each individual who takes on this JOB may emphasize a different area, but each aspect of the JOB must get some attention.

This is the JOB for which I could not be hired, from which I could not be fired, but which I could not quit.

In addition, not because it was part of the JOB but because I got into the swing of things and because I enjoyed it:

- I spent nearly a thousand hours of my own time enhancing the gardens and the grounds of the President's House. I laid out the design for the property, so that it would accommodate both the formal and the informal entertaining that had to be done. I worked in the gardens myself, selected all of the plants and supervised the planting and maintenance of the grounds;
- I worked with the landscape architects hired by the college and was responsible for some improvements in the landscaping around the College, in particular around the new library:
- I developed and ran the Host Family Program for international students, a program that has involved thirty neighborhood families with Babson international students;
- I helped to organize and run (as Chair of the Advisory Committee) the International Student Olympics that for two years brought 400 students from thirteen Boston-area colleges and universities to the Babson College campus for one day of athletic and social events;

- I helped to design and run the orientation program for the wives of Babson international students;
- I helped to select works of art for the new library as a member of the Art Committee;
- I believe I made some contribution to developing a relationship between Babson College and Wellesley College, my alma mater, Class of 1961

OTHER INSTITUTIONS

Each college has its own setting. Each is in a different stage of growth. For each institution and for each time, the needs are different.

The needs of a small, suburban or rural, undergraduate college are different from those of a large, urban, established institution. Amherst, Swarthmore and Babson Colleges have needs that are different from those of Harvard, Boston University or Northeastern.

I believe that the smaller, the more isolated a college is, the younger it is, or the harder that it is trying to grow, the more personal attention it needs. The more it needs people at the top who care about providing informal settings where faculty and students, alumni and trustees and community members can be brought together to get to know one another and to build friendships and trust which will build college spirit, loyalty and pride.

It doesn't matter, perhaps, that at Harvard the current wife of the president has chosen not to be deeply involved in the life of the college in the ways that I have outlined above or that, at the graduate level, at the Harvard Business School, the Dean's wife decided to have little involvement with the school, in fact declined to live in the house on the campus provided by the school.

These institutions are established. There are many built-in ways for their constituencies to communicate. The sense of pride is there and loyalty. Money is flowing in to the development office.

In your search for the new president of Babson College, you, as members of the search committee, will be assuming, whether you are aware of this or not, that the spouse will play a ROLE in representing the college.

You may not be aware, however, of the nature of the JOB that you may be assuming, perhaps unconsciously, that the president's spouse will undertake. The expectation is there, I can testify, even though there will be no job description.

THREE RECOMMENDATIONS

My first recommendation to you as members of the search committee is to decide before you narrow your choice of candidates whether you think that the kinds of service to the college that I have outlined above will continue to be valuable to the college at this stage in its development.

My second recommendation is to be honest not only with your candidates but also with their spouses. Lay your cards on the table early in your discussions.

If you decide that the services outlined above are not essential to the college at this stage in its development, then don't have any expectations. Don't be disappointed if the spouse has a job of her own that demands her full attention. Above all, don't encourage the presidential couple to live in the President's House. The beautiful walls exude tradition—and expectations!

If you decide, on the other hand, that you would like to see a continuation of the kinds of services outlined above, then level with your candidates and their spouses. Respect their need to know and their right to know what you will expect of them—at least your minimum expectations. It will help your candidate and his spouse make an informed decision. It will allow them to consider options:

- If, for example, the spouse has a full-time profession and has no time for the kind of college-related job that she is being asked to do, offer a full staff (which, of course, you would do anyway if there was no spouse.)
  - The president of Wellesley College (a woman) has a permanent housekeeping staff of three.
  - The president of Bryn Mawr College (a woman) hired an executive assistant to supervise and manage her household staff.
- If the spouse is willing but lacks either the physical energy or the necessary administrative and organizational skills for the job that she is being asked to do, be prepared to back up her efforts with a supportive staff.
- If the spouse wants to become involved in some aspects of the job, but not in others, try to accommodate these preferences.

Once you have selected a president, my third recommendation to you as members of the search committee is to suggest that the trustees provide an advocate for the spouse. There should be someone on the board of trustees who is responsible for meeting with the spouse for an hour or so before each meeting of the board to answer questions and to offer support. This person would also be available between meetings and would be able to take information and recommendations from the spouse to the board. The president is not in a position to do this.

Tell that to your candidate and his spouse. But tell them, too, that for the spouse, there will be more than a ROLE to play. There will be JOB to do.

Acknowledge it. Give it dignity.

Chances are that the college will be rewarded by an appreciative presidential couple who will join Babson College with pride in the jobs that they both have been given to do.

Somehow that paper began to circulate. Before long and during the following several years, I received letters from the wives of other college presidents, the wives of headmasters, ministers, athletic coaches, even from a well-known sociologist, thanking me for sharing my experience of being "the-wife-of." They were grateful that someone had validated their lives by writing down the details of that life. Among these letters were several that I mention here:

Angelica Rudenstine, wife of Neal Rudenstine, the President of Harvard University, wrote to me on November 25, 1991:

Thank you so much for sending me your EXCELLENT analysis of the 'role' and the 'job' issue. The trustees of Babson were very lucky to have your experience and your advice, cogently expressed and full of wisdom . . . I would very much like to get together with you one day and talk more about the whole thing. One of your very interesting and (I think) totally original ideas is the trustee advocate for the spouse.

Priscilla K. Gray, wife of Paul Gray, the President of MIT, wrote on November 27, 1984:

I think it is one of the best papers of its kind I have been sent . . . I would be grateful if I might quote you on several of your general points when we retire! (Not quite yet!) You must have made a difference for the one who followed you, and I'm hoping I can do the same. Thank you.

David Riesman, Harvard sociologist and author of *The Lonely Crowd,* (published in 1950) wrote on November 18, 1980. Excerpts:

I am so very grateful to you for your extraordinarily forthright remarks prepared for the Presidential Search Committee . . . While they did not arrive in time for my own talk at the American Association of State Colleges and Universities (a copy of which I enclose,) you will quickly see what strikes me as a remarkable congruence both in whole and in part . . . The London Times Higher Education Supplement would like to publish my talk . . . I would like to revise and improve it . . . I would be grateful for any criticisms that occur to you. (I assume that I cannot properly refer to your own talk at this point, although I would like to do so, if I could.) I wish you could publish what you have written. It is much the most cogent account I have seen of what appear to be the relevant issues . . . . You write with wit and sensibility. Apart from content, it was a pleasure to have a chance to read your comments.

Even Ellen Goodman, American journalist and syndicated columnist for *The Boston Globe*, weighed in with a letter a few years later on April 20, 1987:

> *Dear Mrs. Sorenson,*
> *This should be required reading on the higher education circuit. It's terrific. I hope they took it to heart.*

It is interesting to me that in today's world, women frequently serve as college presidents. I imagine that their spouses or partners expect to continue with their own lives and interests and that the presidential residence is fully managed by a paid professional staff.

On November 3, 1980, two days after I had met with the Presidential Search Committee, Jarvis Farley, Chairman of the Board of Trustees, wrote a confidential memo to the members of the Committee in which he seemed to respond to my remarks:

> *The Committee does not wish to give even the appearance of suggesting that the President must be married or of dictating the role of the President's spouse. With that caveat, the Committee sees two aspects of the spouse's relationships. One is the strengthening support which a spouse gives the President as a personal confidant by sharing understanding of his views and enthusiasm for the mission of the College. The personal role cannot be delegated.*
> *The second aspect involves a multitude of tasks mainly related to College relationships—arranging and hosting College functions, for example, or entertaining distinguished*

visitors, or helping in other important ways as a catalyst in the broad field of relationships among Babson's people. The extent of a spouse's involvement in such matters will depend on the spouse's personal preference and career demands. Such matters can be delegated in whole or in part. The Committee believes that there should be an understanding in advance, with both the President and the spouse, about the expected extent of such involvement."

In the spring of 1981, we said our goodbyes to our many friends at Babson College. I was especially sad to say goodbye to Mike and Jimmy and Edie Sullivan who worked for Buildings and Grounds and with whom I had spent hours caring for the house and the gardens. At a farewell tea, the Babson College Women's Club presented me with a beautiful ode of appreciation, framed and in fine calligraphy, for my contributions to the college. And Betty Farley, wife of the Chairman of the Board of Trustees, wrote a separate piece and presented it to me in a private moment:

When you came, there was a house—tall, well-built, dignified, dark, austere—the President's House. You brought light, color, your personal treasures, warmth into it. You turned the house into a home.

When you came, there were grounds—beautiful, towering trees, plantings near the house, and endless lawn. You studied the grounds, enclosed the lawn from the visibility of the street traffic, planned and planted flowering shrubs along the wall, and designed a flowering divider in the vast lawn. You turned the grounds into a garden.

When you came, there was faculty and staff. Some had been there for years, some were new-comers, and stayed just that. Your husband expanded the faculty, and you brought the newcomers into the group, melded the staff and faculty, and we became a family.

When you came, there were students, many of whom thought college years were golden years for irresponsible play. You received them in your home, and by your courtesy, and graciousness, and genuine interest in them as individuals, you provided them with an example of a fun-loving but responsible adult.

When you came, there were foreign students, from strange lands, and set apart. You brought them together, and they widened their circle of friendships, and we saw them as intelligent, contributing persons. No longer foreigners, they became international students.

You shared your family with us, let us know them, so that they became friends of ours.

All this you did, and more. In all this, you showed your real interest in each individual. You looked on us as persons, not just people. Bless you and thank you.

Thank you, Babson College, I thought at the time, *for all that you have given to Bud, to our family, and to me. We shall never forget you, a wonderful, special community.*

Many years later on February 8, 2019 at a gala event celebrating Babson's Centennial Year, Bud was honored as the College's seventh President by President Kerry Healey, Babson's first female President. While he was President and under his leadership, the College refocused its strategic orientation toward entrepreneurship education and created the world's first

Center for Entrepreneurship Education. Today, Babson College continues to rank as Number One among business schools in terms of entrepreneurship education. Bud's autobiography, published by the College and entitled, *An Entrepreneurial Journey Through Life: Learning, Loving, and Laughing*, was a highlight of the celebration.

Chapter Ten

Cambridge

and the Meadow
(1981–1992)

Lilacs were blooming when we moved from Wellesley back into Cambridge, this time into an historic carriage house on Brattle Street, within walking distance of Harvard Square and the Charles River. A new chapter had begun.

I was forty-two and Bud forty-eight. We would be living together, just the two of us, for the first time in the twenty-one years since our marriage in 1960. Our children had flown the nest. Kristin was now a student at Kenyon College in Ohio. Trina had left the Wellesley High School and planned to spend her senior year as a boarding student at Phillips Andover. Eric was already boarding at Saint Paul's School in Concord, New Hampshire. They subsequently spent their college years, Trina at Princeton and Eric at Yale.

After serving for several years on the company's board of directors, Bud had a new position as CEO of the Barry Wright Corporation. This was a striking change from his years in the academic world.

It was a challenging time for me as well. Even though the city of Cambridge was familiar territory, the world of business was not. Nor was being the wife of a business executive.

I was "the-wife-of" once again, but fortunately for me, this time there were no expectations that I would serve as a social hostess or dedicate my activities to the company. By the early 1980s, wives of business executives had begun leading independent lives with professions of their own.

I loved living in our house in Cambridge, in large part because it was small. After the almost constant entertaining of the Babson years, we could now entertain when we wanted to and only six people at a time. I was also happy because Bud and I now had more time to do things together, even if that meant just walking into Harvard Square to a bookstore or meeting friends at a coffee shop.

We still own the house. It is situated next to the Longfellow House-Washington's Headquarters National Historic Site. Built in 1759, the Longfellow house served during the first year of the Revolutionary War as the headquarters for General George Washington. Subsequently, the poet Henry Wadsworth Longfellow (1807–1882) lived in the house for almost fifty years during which time he built two adjacent houses on Brattle Street for two of his daughters. Our house originally held the carriages and horses used by both daughters.

Behind the Longfellow House and just a few steps from our front door is a period garden with paths bordered by boxwood hedges. It is tended by the National Park Service and is ravishingly beautiful in the spring with foxglove, roses, poppies and delphinium. Planted over two hundred years ago, a majestic linden tree towers over the side lawn, scarlet cardinals singing in its branches.

I decided that I was going to treat this life chapter as a new and exciting adventure, just as I had when living in Europe, Asia, or even while living at Babson. Although I was again in familiar territory, I was determined to seek new challenges. With an empty nest, I knew I would have to be busy. I still ruminated about whether I should focus my efforts to become a professional, but I decided to plunge into doing volunteer work for organizations and causes that I thought were worthy.

For three years, as Chair of Academic Programs for the Wellesley College Alumnae Board, I ran Wellesley's Summer Symposium. I also served on the Alumnae Achievement Awards Committee and on the board of the Students' Aid Society. In 1986, I was Chair of the Twenty-Fifth Reunion for my Wellesley Class of 1961, organizing the event by phone and snail mail, as I didn't yet own a computer.

One afternoon, Dr. Helen Caldicott, a Harvard professor and anti-nuclear weapons activist, spoke at MIT about the dangers of nuclear war which, she said, could lead to the total annihilation of all life on the planet. Hers was an impassioned call to action. I signed on and became the head of the Speakers' Bureau for the Greater Boston Chapter of Physicians for Social Responsibility. At one point, I became so depressed with what seemed to be the inevitable demise of the planet through nuclear warfare that my parents drove from Stockbridge to Cambridge to make sure that my dark vision of the future was not making me sick. I wondered again if it was going to be up to women like Rachel Carson and Helen Caldicott to warn of planetary catastrophes. It still seemed that saving the planet was going to turn out to be a female matter. Were men, with their recognized instincts for aggrandizement and acquisition, jeopardizing the health of the planet? Were women, the stereotypical nurturers, going to be the ones to have to figure out how to save it?

I served as a board member for the Boston Chapter of UNICEF

and as an advisor to the International Wives Group at HBS. I was also a Corporate Trustee of TTOR, The Trustees of Reservations, a conservation organization that preserves land and historic buildings in Massachusetts. Appointed by Edward J. King, Governor of Massachusetts, I was a member for three years of the Board of Trustees for Perkins School for the Blind where Helen Keller had been educated. While there, I was constantly inspired by Helen Keller's words:

> *"The best and most beautiful things in the world cannot be seen or even touched—they must be felt with the heart."*

> *"Life is either a daring adventure, or nothing."*

I was also invited to serve a four-year term on the Ladies Committee at the Museum of Fine Arts, Boston. Following that, for six years, I taught in the Museum's Education Department as a Gallery Instructor. In that capacity, I visited Boston Public Schools in the inner city to educate fifth grade children about the museum and its collections before their class visits to the museum. I loved teaching at the museum, especially in the Egyptian, the Classical Greek, and Roman collections. It seemed like the perfect combination of my interest in teaching and working with children and my background in art history. The Egyptian god, Thoth, and the Greek goddess, Athena, god and goddess of Wisdom, were among my museum friends.

The decade of the 1980s has come to be known as the Reagan Years, conservative and relatively quiet politically, except for the fact that, goaded by President Reagan, the Berlin Wall fell in November of 1989. "Tear down this wall," Reagan had demanded in a speech in West Berlin two years earlier.

In the 1980s Ted Turner started CNN, the 24-hour cable news channel. New technologies, like personal computers and cell phones, were being developed and improved. Bud and I were invited at one point to view one of the early computers at Dartmouth College, a pioneer in the computing world. The early Dartmouth computer was immense, completely filling a large room, floor to ceiling, wall to wall. Driving through the countryside on the way to Hanover, New Hampshire, I couldn't help noticing the cell towers that seemed to be competing with the elegant white spires of the historic churches in New England towns. Were the cell towers now providing the connections and community that had traditionally been provided by the churches?

The black granite Vietnam Veterans Memorial, dedicated to 58,000 veterans, was unveiled in the 1980s. Prince Charles and Lady Diane Spenser were married during that decade.

In 1983, the U.S. put the first American woman, Sally Ride, in space. The space program, however, had its share of tragedies. I remember my shock on January 28, 1986 when I heard the news on the radio that NASA's space shuttle Challenger had exploded almost immediately after lift-off, killing all of the astronauts, among them a woman, a civilian school teacher.

During that decade and, in my opinion, overshadowing all other news, there were three monumental environmental disasters, in India, Russia, and Alaska.

Called the world's worst industrial disaster, a Union Carbide pesticide plant in Bhopal, India accidentally released over forty tons of toxic gases in 1984, instantly killing about 4,000 people and burning and poisoning thousands more. Bhopal is located close to Sanchi, the site of the magnificent Great Buddhist Stupa, a spiritual center constructed by the Emperor Ashoka in the third century B.C. Traveling with a group from the Museum of Fine Arts, Boston, I had visited the Stupa several years before the disaster and had been mesmerized by its beauty. I was heartbroken to think that its physical and spiritual environment had been contaminated with twentieth-century toxic chemicals.

Then there was the Chernobyl nuclear accident in Russia in 1986 and the Exxon Valdez oil spill accident in Alaska in 1989. The corporations involved in these disasters did not seem to suffer remorse or damages nor did they appear to have absorbed the message of Rachel Carson's *Silent Spring*.

Bud and I continued traveling during this decade, searching for Byzantine monasteries on the Greek island of Crete and exploring Japan's historic west coast, its samurai villages, and rustic hot springs. I took my father on a trip to Scotland and Ireland and my mother on trips to Egypt and Mexico. In Merida, my mother and I rented a car and explored Mayan ruins on the Yucatan Peninsula long before there were broad highways and crowds of tourists. We had both read and studied the two-volume *Incidents of Travel in the Yucatan* by John L Stephens and Frederick Catherwood, published in 1841. We were captivated by the work of these two explorers who fought malaria, heat, and exhaustion as they excavated the extensive ancient Mayan network of cities and temples. To celebrate our twenty-fifth wedding anniversary, on June 25, 1985, Bud and I returned to the Hotel Bendinat, our honeymoon hotel, on the Spanish island of Majorca.

There was sadness during the 1980s when we lost beloved members of our family, guiding stars. George Ripley, my father, Verna Sorenson, Bud's mother, and Ralph Sorenson, Bud's father, died within three years of each other.

On November 21, 1989, shortly after Bud and I had taken him to find his ancestral home in Norway, Bud's father, age ninety-one, came to Cambridge from Ohio to spend Thanksgiving with us. I will never forget his words when I picked him up at the airport in Boston. "Do you have everything, Grandpa?" I asked, as we walked toward the car. "Yes, let's see," he responded. "I have my suitcase. I have my hat. And I have my excitement!" We reminisced over dinner about our beautiful trip to Norway. That night Grandpa Sorenson died in his sleep, his excitement intact.

Fifteen years later, my mother died on February 27, 2004 at the age of ninety-two. For her, living was in itself a fine art. She spent her last years living in the Icehouse with my brother Franklin. She knew that he was mentally ill, but she never lost faith in the healing power of love. They were a beautiful pair in those final years, she with dementia, he with schizophrenia, smiling and laughing and complimenting each other. I hesitated to visit too often, fearful that I would upset their delicate relationship.

My grandson Soren, age eight, asked to speak at her memorial service at St. Paul's Church in Stockbridge. Standing in front of a congregation of about 150 townspeople and friends, he calmly adjusted the microphone and started to speak:

> "Last summer," Soren began, "my grandmother, Booma, took my sister Tessa and me to have lunch in the patio of

> the Red Lion Inn across the street from this church. My sister and I ordered lemonade. My grandmother ordered a gin and tonic. When Tessa and I made sipping noises through the straws in our lemonade glasses, my mother told us to stop. She said it was bad manners. We glanced at my grandmother who winked at us, put a straw in her gin and tonic, and began to blow bubbles."

The congregation, having held its collective breath as this poised young boy talked about alcohol, erupted in laughter and applause. After the service, there was a reception at the Lenox Club. When it was over, I went up to the bar to pay the bartender. "I really couldn't figure it out," he said. "Not only did each of the older ladies ask for a gin and tonic; each one wanted a straw! Why was that?" *To blow bubbles, of course,* I thought. What more sparkling tribute could there have been to my effervescent mother. What better memory could she have left for her community to share?

In the late 1980s, something happened in our immediate neighborhood in Cambridge that affected me profoundly. In a legal case that turned out to be a real estate as well as a political scam, we, the City of Cambridge and our immediate neighbors, Jean and Arthur Brooks, were accused of racism by the administration of the Boston-based Commonwealth Day School (CDS) and the Massachusetts District Attorney.

When the property directly adjacent to ours was sold to CDS, we, as abutting neighbors, had raised a zoning objection. CDS planned to turn what had been a small post-high school program for about twenty-five boys into a large school for 150 students. We, as well as the 230 neighbors who signed a petition opposing the school, objected to the traffic, noise and other impacts on the neighborhood that would come from having a much larger school on that property. In response, CDS, citing the fact that the majority of the school's students were black, accused us, Jean and Arthur Brooks and the City of Cambridge of racism. Racial tensions had plagued Boston for years. Our situation significantly increased the tension and was widely reported by the media.

The accusations were deeply hurtful. To me personally, the charge of racism was devastating. I felt that my basic integrity had been attacked. It came as a huge relief when, on June 9, 2004, after years of legal wrangling, Judge Douglas Woodlock, a federal district court judge in Boston, issued a Summary Judgement in which all of the allegations of racism in the case were dismissed. We, as well as the City of Cambridge and Jean and Arthur Brooks, were completely exonerated.

Adding to our relief at having been vindicated, our lawyers also reported that William Walsh, the Cambridge City Councilor and real estate lawyer who had been behind the initial shady real estate dealings of CDS, had been convicted of forty-one counts of bank fraud and sentenced to eighteen months in prison.

During the years of The Case, as I called it, I was alternately astounded, alarmed, strickened, and consumed by the unsupported charges that were levied against us. The lawsuit prompted me to do an immense amount of reading about the law, about an individual's relationship to the legal system, and about how easily a case can be manipulated, shaped and twisted by politicians and the media. I began by reading Franz Kafka's *The Trial*, the chilling story of the experiences endured by Josef K, a man falsely accused of an unspecified crime.

Trying to better understand our situation and feeling that there must be alternatives to litigation as a means of settling disputes, I took a Harvard Law School course in Alternate Dispute Resolution (ADR). I also spent one summer working as a volunteer at the Massachusetts Middlesex County Courthouse in an ADR program called the Multi-Door Courthouse. Both the ADR class and related work gave me tremendous insight into mediation, arbitration, and methods, other than litigation, of defusing tension and handling conflict. And while Bud, Eric and Trina went to Africa one summer to climb Mt. Kilimanjaro, I took public transportation every day to Central Square in Cambridge to study at the Princeton Review. I learned about syllogisms while preparing for the LSAT, the Law School Admission Test. I wanted to understand the law, just in case ADR methods failed. I met with a career counselor at Wellesley College who agreed to support my law school application, if I decided to apply.

Thus over the years in an odd way, The Case went from being a personal nightmare to an opportunity to learn and grow. It was enormously helpful that all of our friends believed in us throughout the ordeal. I was so grateful for that.

During those difficult years, swept up in a cultural narrative over which I felt that I had no control, I often thought of Mary Perkins Bradbury, an ancestor on the True side of the family, whose story I had heard while living as a child with my grandparents in Andover.

During the Salem witch trials of 1692 and 1693, Mary Perkins Bradbury, at the age of seventy-seven, was tried, convicted and sentenced to hang as a witch. She was accused, using spectral evidence, of appearing in the form of a blue boar, thus causing damage to the plaintiff who turned out to be a former rejected suitor seeking revenge. Based on visions and dreams, spectral evidence was allowed in the courts at that time. I was struck in her story by how a prevailing cultural belief can lead to group hysteria and false accusations.

I was incredibly touched by her husband's testimony at her trial. Impressive, too, was the loyalty of her friends and neighbors who themselves, by their association with an accused witch, were at risk of being accused themselves.

Mary spoke first in her own defense on July 28, 1692:

> *"I humbly refer myself to my brethren and neighbors that know me and unto the searcher of all hearts for the truth and uprightness of my heart."*

Thomas Bradbury, Mary's husband, then made the following loving and loyal statement:

> *"Concerning my beloved wife Mary Bradbury this is that I have to say: wee have been married fifty five yeare: and shee hath bin a loveing & faithfull wife to mee, unto this day shee hath been wonder—full laborious dilligent & Industryous in her place and imployment, about the bringing up o'r family (w'ch have bin eleven children of o'r owne, & fower grand-children: shee was both prudent, & provi-dent: of a cheerful Spiritt liberall Charitable: Shee being now very aged & weake, & greived under her affliction may not be able to speake much for herselfe, not being so free of Speach as some others may bee: I hope her life and conversation hath been such amongst her neighbours, as gives a better & more reall Testimoney of her, then can bee exprest by words."*

The supportive testimony of 118 members of her community who had signed a declaration on her behalf made no difference. While awaiting her fate, Mary was incarcerated. Perhaps on the back of another magical blue boar, but more likely with the help of her husband and a bribe for the jailer, Mary escaped from jail. She avoided the noose, it is said, by fleeing in a horse-drawn cart to Maine where she waited out the judges during the witch hunt trials before eventually returning to her community.

In addition to being connected on the True family side to the condemned witch, Mary Perkins Bradbury, we are also connected, on the Ripley family side, to Judge Samuel Sewall (1652–1730), one of the nine judges who sentenced witches to death by hanging. Five years after the witch hunt hysteria had died down, Judge Sewall went into a Boston church and issued an apology for wrongly sentencing a number of men and women. He was the only one of the judges to apologize.

One of the ways that I coped with the stress of the years of The Case was to go back to nature and the land. At some point during the late 1970s, while we were still at Babson, we purchased The Meadow, a house and ten acres of land on Route 183 in Stockbridge, overlooking the rolling Berkshire hills and close to the grounds of the Tanglewood Music Festival. The property included a separate apartment, the Owl's Nest, above a free-standing garage. Our son Eric lived for a year in that apartment while he was teaching at the nearby Berkshire Country Day School. Emanuel Ax, the American classical pianist, put a baby grand piano in the apartment and spent two summers practicing there for his performances at Tanglewood. While the house didn't have a view of the Stockbridge Bowl, our property included a long dirt road that wound down from our house to the lake, a dock, and the boathouse that Eric renovated.

The Meadow was located on the other side of Rattlesnake Mountain from Pilgrims Inn. I relished walking along Rattle-snake Mountain Road, the familiar dirt road that I had traveled so often when I was young. Memories flooded back as I passed the sugaring off shack, the beaver dam, the woodland path to the caves, then up and over the hill to Route 7, bordered on the far side by a stand of hemlocks and beyond it, Pilgrims Inn.

In a way, The Meadow was my salvation. I delighted in working on the house and grounds with Bud, and I exulted in being in close touch with the natural world. Being outside in nature is where I have always felt happiest. I loved gardening and creating magical spots in the landscape. I never tired of admiring the details of flowers and trees or listening to the songs of birds and the wind. I was enchanted to watch the snow falling softly and the flashes of lightning over the hills during summer storms.

For twenty-five years, we spent many weekends and holidays at The Meadow, watching spring turn into summer, then fall and winter, then back into spring. In the meadow in late May, the blossoms on the old apple trees began to drift to the ground and daffodils were replaced by daisies and buttercups. Mountain laurel began blooming in the woods. Closer to the house, Korean lilacs and azaleas began to flower, flickering with bees, butterflies, and hummingbirds.

By mid-June, the peonies and rosa rugosa had stopped bloom-ing, replaced, in the meadow, by Black-eyed Susans and Queen Anne's Lace. We attached bluebird houses to the posts of the fence that lined the dirt road leading to the lake. I loved peeking inside the houses to see the eggs, then the tiny baby bluebirds. Swallows swooped over the meadow attracted by the swallow houses we had placed for them. Red-winged blackbirds sang their beautiful songs above the marshy area at the foot of the meadow harmonizing with the songs of yellow warblers. A black and orange Baltimore oriole built her hanging, pouch-like nest in the ash tree just outside the kitchen window. A robin nested in the euonymus vine beside the front door. In July, yellow daylilies bloomed in the special garden I had created below the meadow. In the fall, the distant hills covered with sugar maples turned into brilliant tapestries of red, orange and gold. At night, the sky above was bright with stars and, during the summer, the meadow twinkled with fireflies.

From the moment we found the house, I dreamed of replacing the dense native plants that dominated the meadow with the waving grasses and wildflowers that I knew filled alpine meadows in the Rocky Mountains. Working before nine in the morning when it became too hot and humid to dig, I enlisted help from the family and tried to create a flower-filled meadow on the two acres of open land between the house and the lake. Armed with shovels, we would go on the attack, ruthlessly digging deep and pulling up the roots of burdock and Canadian thistle, ragweed, bittersweet, and loosestrife, even goldenrod.

The dream was realized. We did create a ravishing wildflower garden, filled with poppies, daisies, coreopsis . . . breathtakingly beautiful. For two summers, we wandered on paths that Bud had cut through the flowers. We made daisy chains and flower crowns for our guests. Then! Nature struck back at our artificial landscape. Clearly, ours was not an alpine meadow. Our New England meadow reverted with a vengeance to a dense field of native weeds, some of which, in revenge for having been attacked, now grew three feet tall. I gave in, relaxed and grew to appreciate the meadow in its natural state. After all, we still had bluebirds, swallows, even a hive of bees. Once in the daylily garden, we watched two foxes on their hind legs holding each other in a mating dance. Deer munched on apples in the old apple orchard.

One summer day when Bud was back at work and the children were at camp or visiting friends, I decided to create a power circle inside an area to the north of our house. I had recently read a study of power circles around the world, places found in mountains, beside lakes, in woods, even in deserts that somehow became natural gathering spots. The common denominator for these circles seemed to be a diameter of nine feet, the perfect diameter for creating a space in which people would feel comfortable talking with others. When seated, they would be not too far from one another (meaning that they would not have to raise their voices to be heard) and not too close, thus risking impinging on someone's personal space.

I put on jeans and a long-sleeved shirt and with an ax and a saw started hacking away at the dense mass of barberry bushes, honeysuckle, and sumac. After a week or so, when the area was cleared of brush, I designed a semi-circular bench of wood with a nine-foot diameter. In front of the bench, the family helped dig a little pool to reflect the sky. We lined it with concrete and surrounded it with maidenhair ferns and spring bulbs. Honey locust trees towered overhead, shading the area and keeping it cool. The power circle with its ferns and spring-flowering plants and its view of distant hills became a popular place to meet.

Over the years, we entertained many of our friends and family on the wide deck that overlooked the meadow and the hills.

From there, we watched the moonrise and the sunrise. Sometimes on windless nights, on our lawn or in our canoe on the lake, we could hear fragments of the concert playing at Tanglewood. From our lawn, we could watch the end-of-the-season fireworks and the brightly colored hot air balloon floating over the hills.

One Tanglewood concert I will never forget. The orchestra was playing Rimsky-Korsakov's *Scheherazade*, inspired by the Middle Eastern tale, *A Thousand and One Nights*. To delay her execution by a wicked king, Scheherazade promised to tell the king an enthralling tale each evening. Sitting on the Tanglewood lawn outside the concert hall, I was myself enthralled, studying the sky as filmy clouds, like Scheherazade's veils, seduced the moon, concealing, then revealing its light, in concert with the swelling and subsiding of the music.

Inside our Berkshire house during the Christmas holidays, Kristin would arrange the furniture and light tiny birthday candles in her dollhouse hidden inside the tall, carved Spanish chest that we had brought from the Philippines. At Thanksgiving, we decorated the long wooden table with candles and bittersweet, once setting the table for thirty guests. Icelandic and Japanese guests arrived from their volcanic islands, wondering if volcanoes had created the Berkshire hills in ages past. The French arrived on their motorbikes, bringing wine.

On June 4, 1994, to celebrate Trina's wedding to Jess Peterson, we erected a large white tent in the meadow. My sister Ginny and her daughter Lucy decorated our canoe with flowers. Then, late in the evening, in a twinkling cloud of fireflies, we paraded down the hill,to the lake following our Scottish friend, Andrew Peterson, playing his bagpipes. Ginny had planted lanterns in the water near the shore. It was a magical scene, as Trina and Jess paddled off through the floating lanterns under the sparkling stars, serenaded by bagpipe music and enthusiastic singing from the wedding guests on the shore.

During our stays in The Meadow, we often saw my parents and my brother Franklin whose hallucinations and symptoms of paranoia were becoming increasingly and distressingly apparent. My bright, witty, fun-loving brother displayed all of the florid symptoms of his mental illness. It was a tragic reality. We treated him gently and with love and respect knowing how much he was suffering. Even Rick Wilcox, the Stockbridge Chief of Police and a childhood friend of Franklin's, respected and supported him. When I once thanked Rick for his help, he said that it was only normal. "We take care of each other in Stockbridge, Charlotte," he said. "We are a family."

My sister Ginny, after losing her husband, moved into an apartment around the corner from our house in Cambridge. She began helping international graduate students from Harvard's Kennedy School with their presentations and their conversational English. Anne, a nurse, returned from three visits to refugee camps in Thailand, helping Cambodian refugees who had fled the terrors of Pol Pot's regime. She was busy setting up a new organization, NPACE, Nurse Practitioners Associates for Continuing Education. My brother George was still in Alaska where he established the Alaska Mountain Wilderness Classic, the world's first and longest cross-country footrace from the town of Hope to Homer. He lived in an octagonal log cabin twenty miles from Homer and in a treehouse when he was in town. A dog team took him into town in the winter, a horse named Aristotle in the summer. Once when our son Eric tried to visit him, he found a note pinned to George's door: "Not Home! Panning for gold!"

One summer, jet skiers discovered the Stockbridge Bowl, their snarling sounds sawing the stillness of the hills during the day and into the evening. I couldn't understand why the right of a single individual to pursue happiness with his jet ski outweighed the right to a peaceful natural environment which constituted the happiness of hundreds who lived in the area. I organized a protest, even going to Boston to an office that had jurisdiction over these matters to request that jet skis be banned from the Stockbridge Bowl. The Town of Stockbridge issued the ban that I believe exists to this day.

Another matter troubled me, a local catastrophe. I learned that the General Electric Company in Pittsfield had been polluting the beautiful Housatonic River with PCB's and other toxic chemicals that might never degrade. It was terrible to realize how careless and destructive we were of our beautiful rivers and land. Would we, the new Stewards of the Land, act in time to save the planet?

One afternoon in the fall, I discovered that by walking from our house, crossing Route 183 and climbing to the top of the ridge known as West Mountain, I had an endless view toward the West. At the time, I never dreamed that I would someday move toward the setting sun to live in Boulder, Colorado, in the foothills of the Rocky Mountains.

Chapter Eleven

Colorado

and a Quest
(1992–2019)

In early July 1992, we left Cambridge and flew to Boulder. The plane climbed a mile in altitude before descending over the flat plains toward the Denver airport. As I looked through the airplane window, I gasped. The words to "America, the Beautiful" came tumbling into my mind:

> *"Oh, beautiful for spacious skies, for amber waves of grain, for purple mountains majesties, above the fruited plain . . ."*
>
> —KATHARINE LEE BATES
> Wellesley College, Class of 1880

The skies were spacious, and the mountains did look purple. Peering from the airplane window, I tried to imagine how the early settlers must have felt when, having crossed the endless great plains in their covered wagons, they looked up and saw the towering mountains, sometimes white with snow. I imagined that the settlers had heated debates around their campfires as they assessed the dangers of trying to cross the mountains. *Why not just stop here and farm this flat, rich land?* said those daunted by the thought of crossing the high mountains. *No,* others insisted. *We must press on. We must.*

As we hit the runway, I knew that living in the West was going to be another great experience. I could feel it.

We settled into our house in Boulder, described at one point in the *Denver Post* as "The little town nestled between the mountains and reality." We chose our house on Mapleton Hill for its location, within walking distance of mountain trails in one direction and of the lively pedestrian center of town in the other. It was easy to slip down to a bookstore or a coffee shop for a cup of hot chai or to walk to the public library or in later years, the Boulder Dushanbe Teahouse, an exquisite gift to Boulder from Dushanbe, Tajikistan, Boulder's sister city.

Our house was surrounded by tall trees—cottonwoods, evergreens, silver maples and an exotic bristlecone pine. It had a view to the south over the area's emblematic Flatirons, a spectacular geologic formation thrusting out of the flat plains. Surprising as it seemed, our Boulder house had been built in 1891, only five years after our historic house in Cambridge.

We were attracted, too, by the Farmers Ditch that flowed through our property. Established in 1862 and one of Boulder's oldest irrigation ditches, it originally flowed year round carrying precious water from the mountains for eight miles to irrigate farmers' fields on the plains. We learned that the cold, fast-flowing water now flows in the Ditch only from late spring to early fall. Praising the beauty and utility of Boulder's extensive network of ditches, Frederick Law Olmsted, Jr., whose father designed Central Park in New York City, studied the landscape in Boulder and in 1910 delivered a report to the city elders that was to serve as a guide to Boulder's growth. He could easily have stood on our property on the bridge that spans the Ditch.

In the mid-1800s when gold was discovered in Boulder Canyon, miners flocked to the area. When settlers first arrived in 1858, they met the Southern Arapaho Chief Niwot (also known as Lefthand) who reportedly told them to leave, saying: "*People seeing the beauty of this valley will want to stay and their staying will be the undoing of the beauty.*" That was called Niwot's Curse. Chief Niwot and the Arapaho and Cheyenne Indians were brutally slaughtered by the U.S. Army in the Sand Creek Massacre in 1864.

The town of Boulder was incorporated in 1871. The University of Colorado opened in Boulder in 1877. In 1898, the Colorado Chautauqua was founded, one of the three out 12,000 original Chautauquas remaining in the United States. It is the site of Colorado's summer music festival.

After we had lived in Boulder for a few months, I wrote the following letter to our friends back in the East:

Dear Friends,

We have arrived! In blue-sky country, a mile closer to the ever-shining sun. We've landed in Boulder, right at the spot where the Great Plains bump firmly into the foothills of the Rocky Mountains. The change from sea level takes your breath away, literally. There is much less oxygen at 5,328 feet. You can remedy this deficit by frequenting a local oxygen bar to inhale a rejuvenating oxygen cocktail.

The air is dry. The lack of humidity means that ferns and mosses don't thrive here, but grasses, succulents, penstemon, Indian paintbrush and the prairie coneflower do.

Yesterday, we picked up a brochure at the entrance to

the Sanitas Trail that gave us instructions about what to do should we encounter a mountain lion. *"Don't panic,"* the brochure advised. *"Don't turn and run. Stay calm. Pick up a rock or a stick. Maintain eye contact with the lion while making yourself as large as possible. Shout and holler. Never crouch or bend over or turn your back on the lion. If you have to move, back up, very, very slowly. Fight back if you are attacked."* I'm not sure if I learned whether to show my teeth or not. Is smiling at a lion a sign of aggression? And, by the way, how can you crouch to pick up a rock or a stick when you are advised to make yourself as large as possible?

We have clearly stepped into a new world with new challenges. This is a good thing! Walks along Brattle Street into Harvard Square were becoming predictable and a little boring. After eleven years in Cambridge, we were ready for a change.

Bud has begun his work as Dean of the Business School at the University of Colorado in Boulder. We plan to spend only a few years here, so we have kept our house in Cambridge, renting out the larger section of the house and keeping a small apartment for ourselves. At first, we were reluctant to move to Boulder, afraid that we might trespass on the lives of our adult children, Trina and Eric, who were already thriving in this beautiful mountain town. They seemed, however, to be enthusiastic about our coming.

I have taken all of my museum clothes—silk blouses, stockings, skirts and heels to Goodwill. I will have no use for East Coast clothes in this land where men and women live in running shoes and fleece jackets and Spandex for the bikers. I haven't seen one man wearing a coat and tie. So far, I haven't seen one woman in a dress. Social events are casual. Not once have I heard anyone ask what school or college I attended or where I summer or where I winter. That is refreshing, liberating, in fact.

Last week, some neighbors invited us to attend a stock show and rodeo near Denver. As I wandered the corridors during intermission, I was incredulous to see that bull sperm was for sale! "Excellent quality! Good prices per liter!" This was not the Boston Flower Show. The Viennese waltz, even square dancing, have been replaced out here by country western music and dancing. We tried it one night at The Grizzly Rose, a dance hall near Denver. Yahoo!

Wellness is a big topic here, maybe because there are so many world-class athletes who like to train at this altitude. Hikers, bikers and walkers flock to Boulder because of the altitude, the 300 days of sunshine and the clean air. I notice that people frequently check their heart rates to see if they are aerobic or anaerobic. There is lots of talk about the best ways to prepare for races. People exchange information about holistic doctors who treat the whole body, often by prescribing herbs or acupuncture or meditation. One is advised to take responsibility for one's own health and not unquestioningly to take the word of practitioners of allopathic medicine who are likely to prescribe *toxic* pharmaceutical drugs with their complicating side effects.

The Mediterranean Diet is recommended for good health. People try to eat organic fruits and vegetables, locally produced.

I find that Boulder is full of *healers*, each using a different healing modality. There are so many healers that I wondered at first who in the city was left to heal. Then I realized that the healers were healing each other. This focus on holistic healing and physical and spiritual wellness is so different from the intense intellectualism that characterizes Cambridge.

Politically, Boulder is progressive, very much like Cambridge. In fact, like Cambridge, it is known as a People's Republic.

I am excited to be here! It truly is a new adventure! Come and visit! You will see.

Love and Light,

Charlotte

(Out here, by the way, everyone calls me Chaco, after my love of Chaco Canyon and chocolate, I guess.)

P.S. The local newspaper reported this morning that a resident used an antique sword to scare off a mountain lion that was attacking his dog. I thought that antiques could only be found in the East. Not true! Also, everyone in Boulder seems to have at least one dog.

P.P.S. Lest you think that we are culturally deprived, Boulder, with its population of interesting, highly educated people, has rich musical and theatrical offerings, bookstores and stimulating courses offered at the University of Colorado.

P.P.P.S. "How do you feel about the move?" So many of you have asked. I can only answer that I feel like an epiphyte. What is that? It is a plant, like an orchid, that lives on another plant. Its roots dangle. That is the way I feel out here. I love the sun. I enjoy the view, but when I look down from my high mountain perch, I can see, and I can feel, that I have no roots, at least no roots in the ground!

Even after moving to Boulder, Bud and I continued our travels here and there around the world. Together on a whim, under a full moon and without a guide, the two of us climbed Mt. Fuji (13,333 feet) one hot August night, arriving at the summit just as the red sun was rising over Japan. We canoed once through pods of hippos on the Zambezi River in Zimbabwe and were with the first group to canoe the rushing rivers of northern Iceland. Twice, we rode Icelandic ponies with Icelandic friends (who spoke Old Norsk) through the wild interior of Iceland. On two visits to New Zealand, we rented a sloop and, without being seasoned skippers, ventured into the rocky strait between the North and South Islands, feasting on green-lipped mussels that Bud pulled off the rocks and quickly learning how to anchor in ten-foot tides. We spent wonderful holidays with the whole family in Mexico, Ecuador, and Costa Rica.

Traveling alone, I once spent a month in a language school in Antigua, Guatemala, studying Spanish. On another occasion, I packed a suitcase with books on Ancient Greece and spent a few weeks by myself in Athens, reading my books at night and exploring the city during the day. A few years ago with a group of university women, I met with professional women in Jordan and discussed their problems with Sharia law: "*Until women are allowed, with male jurists, to interpret Sharia law, there will be no meaningful progress for women in the Islamic world.*" With the same group, I met professional women in Cuba who spoke about the problems they faced living under a Communist regime. "*We can't leave the country. We live here like prisoners. We have ration cards. If we speak against the government, we will be jailed.*" Before arriving we had been told to clean our computers of any reference to Cuba. We were monitored everywhere we went. Every meeting room, even our bus, was bugged.

I was fifty-three when we moved to Boulder and I had never considered that life is a Journey, a personal, spiritual exploration. Someone asked me shortly after we arrived where I was on my Journey. I had absolutely no idea what he was talking about. "Hmm . . . well," I responded, not understanding the question, "we have just moved here from Cambridge, Massachusetts."

In terms of a personal life design, if in fact I had considered the matter at all, I thought of a person's life to be divided into chapters. I had never imagined each of us being on a personal journey with the opportunity to create a life, including a spiritual life.

Moving, I found, was a good opportunity to refresh my thinking. I knew when I was packing to leave the East that I had resolved my conflict between choosing to be a homemaker or a paid professional. I was leaving Betty Friedan behind. I no longer yearned to go to law school. I had found my balance in that regard and was content with the life choices that I had made and was making.

Also while closing my suitcase, I made a conscious decision not to accept invitations in Boulder to join committees or boards. I had done so much of that in the East. When I finally settled in Boulder, with the exception of starting a pedestrian advocacy organization called Walk Boulder and helping with another effort to encourage organic agriculture in Boulder County, I tried to keep my calendar free of volunteer commitments.

Instead, intrigued by the idea of life as a journey, I was eager to explore the spiritual side of life. I set out to seek Enlightenment. Over my lifetime, having lived in distant places and traveled to many countries, I knew that people hold distinctly different religious and cultural beliefs. I had come to realize that I could not accept a single over-arching belief system like Christianity or one of its many denominations. I had often asked myself, for example, how I could call myself an Episcopalian and believe in the Trinity when I had traveled in India where worshippers can make a choice from among hundreds of gods? How could I believe in the exclusive sanctity of Jesus and the Bible after visiting Muslim countries like Morocco, Egypt, Turkey and Jordan where the Koran is considered the sacred word of God revealed directly to Mohammed, the last of the prophets. In those countries, Christ is considered a mere prophet, not the Son of God.

Or why wouldn't I begin to question organized religion itself after traveling to places like Angkor Wat in Cambodia where Buddhist priests in their saffron robes wander in ruined Hindu temple complexes, chanting mantras of renunciation? What about people who still follow the ancient and animistic Shinto beliefs in Japan and worship Kami at Shinto Shrines? I began to wonder if the Communists in secular China practice a religion: atheism? Or is capitalism perhaps a form of religion?

Of course, I understood then that organized religions around the world satisfy the compelling need in all individuals to identify with a community where they can share beliefs, traditions, ceremonies and rituals. And organized religions often satisfy the profound human need for sanctuaries, places of peace and beauty and safety where one can contemplate life's wonders and mysteries, places that also can witness, and hold and understand deep emotions like grief and pain.

Today, if I had to name my chosen place of worship, I would say, *"Nature is my temple."* And if I had to give a name to my religion, I would say, as the Dalai Lama says, *"Kindness is my religion."* At least, it is my aspiration.

In any case, I decided to seek spiritual enlightenment in a conscious, focused way. On a number of occasions, I set off from Boulder and drove four hours south to Crestone, Colorado. Only one block square, this tiny town lies at the foot of the Sangre de Christo Mountains, peaks that rise 14,000 feet on the eastern side of the San Luis Valley, a vast high desert valley. Worshippers of many faiths including Tibetan Buddhists, Hindus, Native Americans, Catholics, Protestants and Christian mystics, all have found in Crestone an energy vortex, a particular vibrant Earth energy. The area has become a spiritual mecca, home to more than two dozen ashrams, monasteries, temples, retreat centers, stupas and other sacred places, even a ziggurat and a Japanese center for sustainable agriculture.

I was fortunate to be in Crestone in the fall of 2007 for the first, and maybe the only, Sacred Peaks Enlightenment Conference. The leaders of all of the area's diverse spiritual traditions gathered one evening to explain their different practices. I listened carefully, hoping to be inspired, but I wasn't drawn to any single leader or practice. The practices, as described that night by their leaders, seemed to me to be either too rigid, too academic, too complicated, or, even for me, too strange.

Near the end of the presentation, the leader of the Native American group in Crestone spoke. "I feel tired and lost inside a building. My home is in Nature. I embrace the strength and wisdom of trees. They talk to me. I don't need a preacher. Animals share their wisdom. Plants provide beauty and food. The air is clean and cool. The sun warms. The stars shine. The moon glows. My soul is full." At last! His words resonated with me. His was a belief system that I could embrace. "Nature is not only my place of worship," he continued in his deep voice, "but it is my inspiration and spiritual guide. It is my religion."

As I listened, I knew that I have always found my spiritual sanctuary in nature, not in a church or a cathedral, impressive as they might be. For me, both the swamp where I had celebrated my eleventh birthday and the woods on Rattlesnake Mountain in the Berkshire Hills were rich and pulsing with life. Both the swamp and the mountain were to me magical and nourishing places, sacred places. I was deeply happy when I was there. Academics or theologians might say that I found spiritual renewal in those places because I felt part of the Oneness of All Things. All I know is that during times when I am alone in Nature, in the wetlands and the woods, on mountain tops, on the sea or in open spaces, I feel fully content and complete and full of joy.

Along with two other conference attendees, I climbed into a Jeep early the following morning. We drove for a full day over bumpy mountain roads to visit the spiritual centers we had learned about the night before. Each center was hidden from view from the road, and each was unique, but, except for the Japanese Zen Center, I didn't feel drawn to any of these places of worship.

I made friends in Crestone, drinking hot chai at the Shambala Café and staying at a small inn around the block. Over the years, whenever they knew that I planned to visit, the innkeepers saved a special corner room for me. They even painted it the color of bittersweet, saying that that was my color.

On one visit, I met Jeremiah at the Shambala Café, not the Biblical prophet but a twenty-two-year-old American hippie with dreadlocks and a snaggletooth. We began talking about gurus. I said that I had never met one, but that I would like to. Emphatically, he protested: "Charlotte, you have no need to seek a guru. The only guru you will ever need is inside of you, in the calm, still place within you, within everyone."

"In Stillness There is a Song." Jeremiah's words made me think of my inscription in the meditation retreat that I had designed on the shore of Lake Waban on the Wellesley College campus. I think of the word "Still" as pulsing with life. Jeremiah's "calm, still place within everyone" is for me quiet, but alive and full of promise.

In 2007, I traveled for three weeks in India with an international group of Sufis. I had been invited to join the group by a friend who herself was a Sufi. Sufis practice the mystical form of Islam, each day chanting the ninety-nine names of Allah. They believe in an individual's inward search for Beauty, Love and Joy. The following are excerpts from my journal:

> We travel with Swami Sundaranand, a Holy Man, clad in a pale apricot and orange robe. He is an older man, tall and substantial with a gray beard and ponytail and three saffron lines of sacred ash marking his forehead. His home is in Gangotri in the Himalayas at the headwaters of the sacred river Ganges. For eight hours in a featureless bus, we wind our way for 230 kilometers arriving finally at an ancient temple dedicated to the powerful Hindu god Shiva, Creator and Destroyer.
>
> In my room that first night, a single fluorescent bulb hangs from the ceiling. The mattress is one inch thick on a wooden bedframe. Sheets are a scratchy synthetic fabric, black with beige and brown flowers. I will sleep on them for a week. A plastic pail and a red ladle serve as a shower in the tiny adjacent bathroom. There is cold water from a spigot on the wall. There are no towels, so I dry off under the ceiling fan that has one speed, low. There is no screen

on the bathroom window. Mosquitos hum. The toilet leaks. The sink is filigreed with a spider web holding a massive spider. In good Jain fashion and in the spirit of *ahisma* or non-violence, I will not kill it. I am thoroughly exhausted.

The lights suddenly go out. The ceiling fan stops. With my flashlight, I can see a battalion of tiny ants demolishing my securely-wrapped protein bar on the shelf. A cockroach scuttles across the floor. I lie there in the dark, bewildered. Who are the Sufis and what do they believe? And why is this group of Muslim Sufis here at this ancient Shiva temple, a sacred pilgrimage site for Hindus? And why in the world am I here? Just raw curiosity? What indeed am I looking for?

Every morning at six, the Swami sits down cross-legged on a cushion on the balcony. For three hours, we meditate, focusing on the third eye. We chant "Om Namah Shivaya" and we practice breathing. I am distracted by the monkeys on the balcony and I am restless. The Swami moves his fingers slowly along the beads of his mala. After 108 beads there is a red tassel. The Swami starts fingering the beads again. I watch closely, hoping that he will finish by the next red tassel. I am eager for a cup of hot chai. At the end of the meditation, the Swami touches the beads to his right eye, his left eye, his third eye, then his heart. I secretly wonder what value there is when a whole culture—swamis, gurus, sadhus and sannyasin—meditates so much of the day. A heretical thought.

I also wonder why I have come all the way to India to seek enlightenment, India with its caste system, its dowry system, its mainly illiterate and superstitious population, its brutal treatment of women and the Untouchables, its unrelenting poverty and multitudinous gods? Why am

I seeking spiritual enlightenment in a culture built on this foundation?

One day I talk with Carmen, a warm, intelligent, strong-minded, creative, giving woman who lives fully from the heart. She says that Sufis try to find the Beauty in each person they meet, the Radiance. 'Find the radiant spot within yourself and reflect it outwards,' she says. 'Be kind. Have a happy heart. Raise that vibration.' A wasp settles on her pants. She gently guides it onto her paper plate and lets it feed on her lunch.

After a week, we say our farewells to Swami Sundaranand. Several men kneel and put their hands, then their foreheads on the Swami's sandaled feet. They then place their sanctified hands, first on their own foreheads, then upon their hearts.

"*Swaha*," the Swami intones, "So be it."

At the Ananda Ashram in the village of Kanhangad, about three hours by bus south of Mangalore, devotees come from around the world to meditate and find their bliss. From dawn until ten in the evening, they repeat a chant, a tribute to Ram, one of the manifestations of the Hindu god Vishnu.

"Om Sri Ram Jai Ram Jai Jai Ram . . . Om Sri Ram Jai Ram Jai Jai Ram . . . Om Sri Ram Jai Ram Jai Jai Ram."

We meet Swami Muktananda, the head of the ashram. He is a powerfully built, handsome, intelligent man in his early sixties. I hear that he is a prodigious reader and that he lives alone in a small hut and sleeps on the floor. He is dressed in an orange robe.

"In stillness," the Swami preaches during an afternoon Satsang, "you will know and understand God. Through chanting, we enter into the perfect stillness deep within us.

We dissolve the ego and become one with everyone and everything, with every animal, plant, rock, bird. Behold God in your own heart, then behold God everywhere."

Was I Enlightened, after this visit to India? Made One with the Universe? Witness to the Ultimate Truth? No, I regret to say. I remained a seeker. I was heartened, however, to find that Crestone Jeremiah's message as well as that of the Hindu Swamis seem to be the same, "*The wisdom you seek is within you." Swaha!*

Some winters, when Boulder was slippery with snow and ice, Bud and I would visit Tulum in the Yucatan, Mexico. Bud would usually follow that short visit with a trip to the Philippines for a board meeting of the Asian Institute of Management. I would return alone to Boulder.

One year on our last day in Tulum, I walked the beach as usual at sunrise, watching the golden sun rise out of the ocean and thinking about facing cold weather and colorless gardens in Boulder. Suddenly, I stubbed my toe on a wooden board half-hidden in the sand. *For Rent.* I looked up and saw, right there on the beach, a most magical shack with a thatched roof. There was no way that I was going to return to Boulder. I stayed. And I came back year after year to live for a month or two in that magical shack, La Casa Amor, on the sea. In letters to Bud, I tried to capture some of my experience:

How I love it here in this light-filled world! Last night the moon rose, full, brassy and cold. This morning when I started my beach walk at six, I was embraced and protected by a pale golden disc rising in the east and a pale silvery disc sliding to the horizon to the west. The wind swaying the coconut palms, the sound of the waves, the soft white powdery sand, pelicans flying overhead. I am in heaven.

It is early evening now, and I am sitting in the magical shack. I have lit an incense stick. The fragrance of copal fills the air. I love living by myself on this talcum powder beach in this thatched hut fashioned of driftwood. Waves crash onto the shore, just steps away. The waves are light-filled, celadon, jade, lapis lazuli and turquoise, with snowy crests. The sea is polished silver, turning to pewter, then, almost black. Sometimes the distant horizon disappears into the clouds. Then the sky and the sea are one, indistinguishable, waves and clouds, swirling and foaming. Here and there along the powdery beach, I can see stubby peninsulas of black jagged rocks jutting into the sea, immovable, defiant. The celadon and lapis waves foam and swirl around them, soft, fluid, flexible.

Wind whistles through the cracks in the walls of this thatched house on the beach. It whirls through the crescent and the star carved into the wooden door. Wind slithers under the house, too, and up between the floorboards. Feathers hanging from the dream catchers on the ceiling catch the wind. The house sways gently on its stilts like a boat at anchor.

Another year, I wrote:

I am loving every moment of this solo retreat: the chance to walk and walk on the endless beach and to live in rhythm with the sunrise and the sunset and with the rain, even the rain that pours through the thatched roof of the magic shack. To live gently and quietly and to live, except occasionally, without electricity and TV and a telephone and a car and all of the techno-trapping of our "advanced" culture. What a blessing! What freedom!

My neighbors Paco (Mexican) and Lucia (Italian) are treasures. Paco tells me, "You have found an anchor here for your soul." Paco and Lucia live simply on the beach, appreciating everything, blessing everything. Lucia, laughing joyously and gilded with sunshine, makes a celebration out of washing her single cooking pot every morning in the surf.

Maria, the Mexican ballerina and creator of the magical shack has just flown out of her tiny round palapa kitchen, laughing, her long black hair flying behind her. Laughing, too, Italian Simone who looks like Apollo, bursts from the kitchen and chases her at top speed along the talcum-powder beach. Apollo and Daphne in a seaside romp. Happy. Innocent.

I attend a ceremony in a sweat lodge. There are nine of us, nine women. Except for the soft-spoken shaman, Pedro, there is only feminine energy in the lodge, feminine vibrations. We sit on the palm fronds that cover the sandy floor. It is dark, except for the glow from the embers in the fire pit in the center of the circular structure. Pedro, the shaman, chants softly, Mayan chants. His voice is haunting, a soft wail, coming, it seems, from another time and place, from the soul of the earth. *"Earth is our body; Water, our blood; Air, our breath; Fire, our spirit."*

With reverence Pedro sprinkles incense on the molten rock in the fire pit. The air is filled with an exotic fragrance.

In the darkness and quiet, we meditate, then each states an intention. Most have to do with finding hope or a path or a way to give. Later we express gratitude for families, for friendships, for beauty. "I am grateful for the Darkness," someone murmurs, "for without Darkness, we would not know Light." The Mayan shaman says softly, *"Aho!"* So be it.

I have started wearing feather earrings and a beaded anklet, a red headband, and a long, silky Indian skirt. I meet such unusual and interesting people on the beach. (I probably look pretty unusual myself!) Is this an echo of what I felt when I was young and living with artists and actors and musicians and dancers and LAUGHTER at Pilgrims Inn?

Trina, Kristin, and Eric, but not you, Bud, are worried about my infatuation with this place. Trina says that she is coming to check on me, to make sure that I haven't gone crazy, especially to make certain that I don't plan to get a tattoo!

They don't have to worry. I'm fine. I feel open and free and so at one with the risings and settings of the sun and the moon, with the shining stars, the wind, the salty tang in the air, the sound of waves crashing against the rocks, with the dainty sandpipers skittering in the iridescence where the sea retreats from the sand, with the pelicans flying in military formation above the palms. I feel alive and full of love and joy. Maybe this feeling, this joyful vibration, is what I was seeking when I set out on my quest for enlightenment. I will try to sustain it. In any case, I know that, from now on, when searching for wisdom and guidance, I will always trust that still place in my heart. *Swaha!* and *Aho!* I say to myself. *So be it.*

We have loved living in Boulder for the past twenty-seven years, meeting and getting to know a number of special people. A Persian myth defines Paradise as a Garden! One of the most interesting and talented people I have met in Boulder is Sina Simantab, originally from Iran, who not only has created a garden paradise at the Highland City Club but has also created there a vibrant community of creative people. Gathered once a week around a wooden refectory table in the library are the participants in member Steve Smith's weekly discussion group. With his fine intelligence, sense of irony, and enthusiasm for unearthing and introducing provocative subjects, Steve is the City Club's Socrates. *"I cannot teach anybody anything. I can only make them think,"* said the fifth-century B.C. philosopher. With his elegantly-crafted introductions to a wide variety of topics, Steve makes me think. I always regret when I have to miss one of his discussions.

My deepest pleasure during these years has been sharing in the lives of our children and our grandchildren, some of whom live in Boulder. I have loved family celebrations, skating and sledding with Eric and Jeannine, Emily and Felix above the Flatirons and hiking and canoeing with Trina and Jess, Soren and Tessa on Glacier Lake near Nederland, a mountain town above Boulder. We feel the same happiness when we visit Kristin and Eric Stark's children, Will and Sophie, Alexa and Evan, in Garrison, New York and in Waldoboro, Maine.

By far, the greatest blessing of these years has been to have shared my life with Bud, my extraordinary husband. Bud has been an incredible companion, as we have journeyed together through life. *"Traveling with Bud is a lark!"* I wrote in my journal in 1992 when we were exploring New Zealand. *"He is fun and funny, thoughtful, sensitive, flexible, intelligent, resourceful, a planner (but not too much), warm and loving, gentle and generous, infinitely curious, enthusiastic, consistent, patient, and kind, appreciative of genuine human virtue, interested in everything. He has an eye for beauty and an awareness of the universals. And much, much more. Handsome, too!"*

Next year, we will celebrate our sixtieth wedding anniversary. Salman Rushdie recently defined a lasting marriage: *"It takes patience, understanding, determination, passion, tenderness, tough-mindedness, originality, desire, imagination and love, above all, love."* All true. I would add that it also takes respect, trust, loyalty, dependability, tact, humor, and lots of luck.

Epilogue

I gaze once again at the stained glass scene that Charlotte, my grandmother, fashioned so long ago with the apple tree arching over the cobalt blue pond, the scene that inspired me to attempt to write the story of my life's eighty-year journey. As I study it, the cobalt blue pond seems deeper now with its rich accumulation of memories. And the ripples on the surface of the pond carrying messages of Beauty, Love, and Joy seem to be expanding outwards into the lives of my children and grandchildren, as they discover their songs and begin to create their own life journeys.

Acknowledgements

My gratitude extends

—to those ancestors and forebears whose life stories influenced my own,

—to those teachers who continue to inspire me with their knowledge, wisdom, and personal example,

—and to dear friends who read the first few chapters of my story and encouraged me to continue—Sally Barrett-Page, Barbara Barss, Lee Carlin, Deborah Cassady, Martha Mel Edmunds, Anne Groves, Muni Fluss, and Willinda McCrea.

Most of all, I am grateful to my husband and children who know my story and who understood what I was trying to put into words. Their love and encouragement while I wrote my remembrances meant everything to me. I am especially indebted to my daughter Kristin whose editorial guidance was exceptional.

For their support, patience, and creative solutions to publishing problems and for their positive assurances that there would be, in the end, a book, I am also grateful to:

Aaron Perry, Publishing Manager
Maggie McLaughlin, Design Director
Jake Welsh, Cover Art Director